OCS Study
MMS 2004-070

User's Guide for the 2005 Gulfwide Offshore Activities Data System (GOADS-2005)

I0439051

Final Report

U.S. Department of the Interior
Minerals Management Service
Gulf of Mexico OCS Region

OCS Study
MMS 2004-070

User's Guide for the 2005 Gulfwide Offshore Activities Data System (GOADS-2005)

Final Report

Authors

Darcy Wilson
Andy Blackard
Stephanie Finn
Eastern Research Group, Inc.
Morrisville, North Carolina

Brian Boyer
COMM Engineering, Inc.
Lafayette, Louisiana

Prepared under MMS Contract
1435-01-04-CT-31021
by
Eastern Research Group, Inc.
1600 Perimeter Park Drive
Morrisville, North Carolina 27560

Published by

U.S. Department of the Interior
Minerals Management Service
Gulf of Mexico OCS Region

New Orleans
October 2004

DISCLAIMER

This User's Guide was prepared under contract between the Minerals Management Service (MMS) and Eastern Research Group, Inc. This User's Guide has been technically reviewed by the MMS and approved for publication. Approval does not signify that the contents necessarily reflect the views and policies of the MMS, nor does mention of trade names or commercial products constitute endorsement or recommendation for use. It is, however, exempt from review and compliance with the MMS editorial standards.

REPORT AVAILABILITY

Extra copies of this report may be obtained from the Public Information Office (Mail Stop 5034) at the following address:

U.S. Department of the Interior
Minerals Management Service
Gulf of Mexico OCS Region
Public Information Office (MS 5034)
1201 Elmwood Park Boulevard
New Orleans, Louisiana 70123-2394

Telephone: (504) 736-2519 or
           1-800-200-GULF

CITATION

Suggested citation:

Wilson, D., A. Blackard, S. Finn, and B. Boyer. 2004. User's Guide for the 2005 Gulfwide Offshore Activities Data System (GOADS-2005): Final Report. U.S. Dept. of the Interior, Minerals Management Service, Gulf of Mexico OCS Region, New Orleans, LA. OCS Study MMS 2004-XXX. 90 pp.

TABLE OF CONTENTS

Section   **Page**

LIST OF FIGURES vii

1. INTRODUCTION 1-1

    1.1   Principles of Use and System Requirements.. 1-1

    1.2   Installation 1-1

2. USING THE 2005 GULFWIDE OFFSHORE ACTIVITIES DATA SYSTEM
    (GOADS-2005).. 2-1

    2.1   Starting and Exiting GOADS-2005... 2-1

    2.2   Creating and Editing Data 2-8

         2.2.1   Creating and Editing Structure Data...................................... 2-8

         2.2.2   Creating and Editing Equipment Data.................................... 2-13

    2.3   Quality Control Tests 2-15

    2.4   Saving and Backing Up Work.. 2-16

    2.5   Setting Status of Facilities and Equipment... 2-17

    2.6   Finding Help and Extra Information 2-17

3. UPON SURVEY COMPLETION.. 3-1

    3.1   How, When, and Where to Deliver Data Files.. 3-1

    3.2   Failed Quality Control Tests 3-1

    3.3   QA Summary Form 3-1

APPENDIX A: HELP TEXT FILES A-1

    A.1   User Information A-3

    A.2   Structure Information A-4

    A.3   Amine Gas Sweetening Unit A-6

    A.4   Boiler/Heater/Burner.. A-10

    A.5   Diesel or Gasoline Engine A-13

    A.6   Drilling Rig A-16

    A.7   Combustion Flare.. A-18

    A.8   Fugitives... A-20

    A.9   Glycol Dehydrator Unit A-23

    A.10 Loading Operation A-28

    A.11 Losses From Flashing A-30

    A.12 Mud Degassing A-32

    A.13 Natural Gas Engine A-33

TABLE OF CONTENTS (CONTINUED) ·

                                                                                  Page

A.14   Natural Gas Turbine A-36
A.15   Pneumatic Pumps A-39
A.16   Pressure/Level Controllers A-41
A.17   Storage Tank A-42
A.18   Cold Vent A-46

APPENDIX B: GOADS-2005 QA SUMMARY FORM DATA FIELDS B-1

LIST OF FIGURES

Figure   **Page**

2-1   Populating GOADS-2005.. 2-2

2-2   New User Screen 2-3

2-3   GOADS-2005 Main Window.. 2-3

2-4   GOADS-2005 Main Menu 2-5

2-5   GOADS-2005 Help Menu 2-6

2-6   GOADS-2005 Import Screen 2-7

2-7   GOADS-2005 Export Screen 2-8

2-8   New Structure Dialog Box 2-9

2-9   Structure Screen in Description Edit Mode.. 2-10

2-10   Structure Screen in Activity Edit Mode 2-11

2-11   Sales Gas Screen 2-12

2-12   New Equipment Dialog Box 2-14

2-13   QC Results Tab 2-16

3-1   QA Summary Form Screen 3-2

1. INTRODUCTION

The Minerals Management Service (MMS) mandated that offshore operators in the Gulf of Mexico participate in an annual survey program for the years 2000 and 2005. For 2000, MMS collected information regarding offshore operations. The purpose of the survey was to assist the MMS in constructing an emission inventory for the entire Gulf of Mexico. For the 2000 inventory effort, MMS funded the development of the Gulfwide Offshore Activities Data System (GOADS-2000) software in order to assist offshore operators in complying with the MMS mandate. The GOADS software assists users in recording information regarding emissions-related offshore activities and generates computer data files that can be delivered to the MMS. For the 2005 inventory effort, significant improvements have been made to the original software; the new version is GOADS-2005. The GOADS-2005 software will be used to record information regarding emissions-related offshore activities for calendar year 2005.

For 2005, the GOADS-2005 software has been reengineered to simplify data entry to focus on activities that change monthly. The primary difference between the 2000 GOADS and the GOADS-2005 is that platform descriptive data as well as the equipment descriptive data only need to be entered once, not every month. The GOADS-2005 still includes the QA Summary Form that needs to be printed out and submitted with the activity data file(s).

1.1   PRINCIPLES OF USE AND SYSTEM REQUIREMENTS

The GOADS-2005 works on IBM-compatible personal computers (PCs) that are equipped with the Microsoft Windows® 98, NT, or XP operating systems. The user should possess a modest familiarity with the Windows operating environment and should understand a few of its common features, such as point-and-click, file management, menu-driven selection, and text boxes.

1.2   INSTALLATION

The GOADS-2005 distribution pack includes this User's Guide; lookup tables with MMS information such as operator IDs and other structure data, and an Installation CD (GOADS-2005). The lookup tables and Installation CD are necessary to complete the installation of GOADS-2005.

Complete the following steps to install GOADS-2005:

1. Insert the Installation CD into the CD-ROM (assumed here to be the d:\ drive).

2. Click ▦Start from the Windows Taskbar, then select ▦.

3. Type d:\GOADS-2005.msi (CD ROM) and click OK.

4. Follow the instructions that appear on each successive screen, and click Finish to complete the installation.

   During the installation process, the setup program may ask you to reboot your machine one or more times (depending upon the files currently installed on your PC). You should reboot when asked.

5. Remove the Installation CD.

6. The Installation CD should be stored in a safe place.

2. USING THE 2005 GULFWIDE OFFSHORE ACTIVITIES DATA SYSTEM (GOADS-2005)

The GOADS-2005 software assists users in completing monthly surveys covering air emissions-related activities that are associated with offshore facilities. GOADS-2005 queries the user regarding emissions-related operating data, saves the data on the user's PC, and guides the user to create copies of the data on floppy disks or compact disks (CDs) for backup or delivery to the MMS. Figure 2-1 presents a flowchart that describes the steps in populating the GOADS-2005 database.

- You should run GOADS-2005 in order to enter new operating data for each month. For example, if production or throughput volumes change from month-to-month, this new information should be entered for every month. Parameters that remain constant do not need to be entered every month.

- A saved data set corresponding to one month is called a "survey" or a "monthly survey." Upon creating a survey, you should enter information that represents your offshore facility and all emissions-producing equipment on the facility. GOADS-2005 provides a "fill-in-the-blank" approach in order to generate structure, equipment, and production/throughput data.

- As you enter data, GOADS-2005 performs a number of automatic error checks. If an error is suspected, you will be reminded and may be asked to correct the error or provide comments in a text box. After the data are submitted, MMS will attempt to reconcile missing or unusual data by reviewing the comments or contacting you by telephone. GOADS-2005 performs the following types of error checks:

  - ☑ Completeness – to identify missing data entries

  - ☑ Range – to determine when data entries fall outside of typical ranges

  - ☑ Consistency – to determine whether data entries are consistent with one another

  - ☑ Month-to-month – to determine whether information that typically varies by month has been reviewed and edited appropriately or to flag items that change radically from one month to the next

2.1 STARTING AND EXITING GOADS-2005

To start GOADS-2005, click ▥ Start from the Windows taskbar, then select Programs ▸ | GOADS-2005. Upon starting GOADS-2005 for the first time, the "New User" screen will appear (Figure 2-2). At this point you must fill in the requested contact information in order to proceed. You will only need to complete this screen once. The next time you run GOADS-2005, it will NOT appear. Instead, the Main Window (Figure 2-3) will appear.

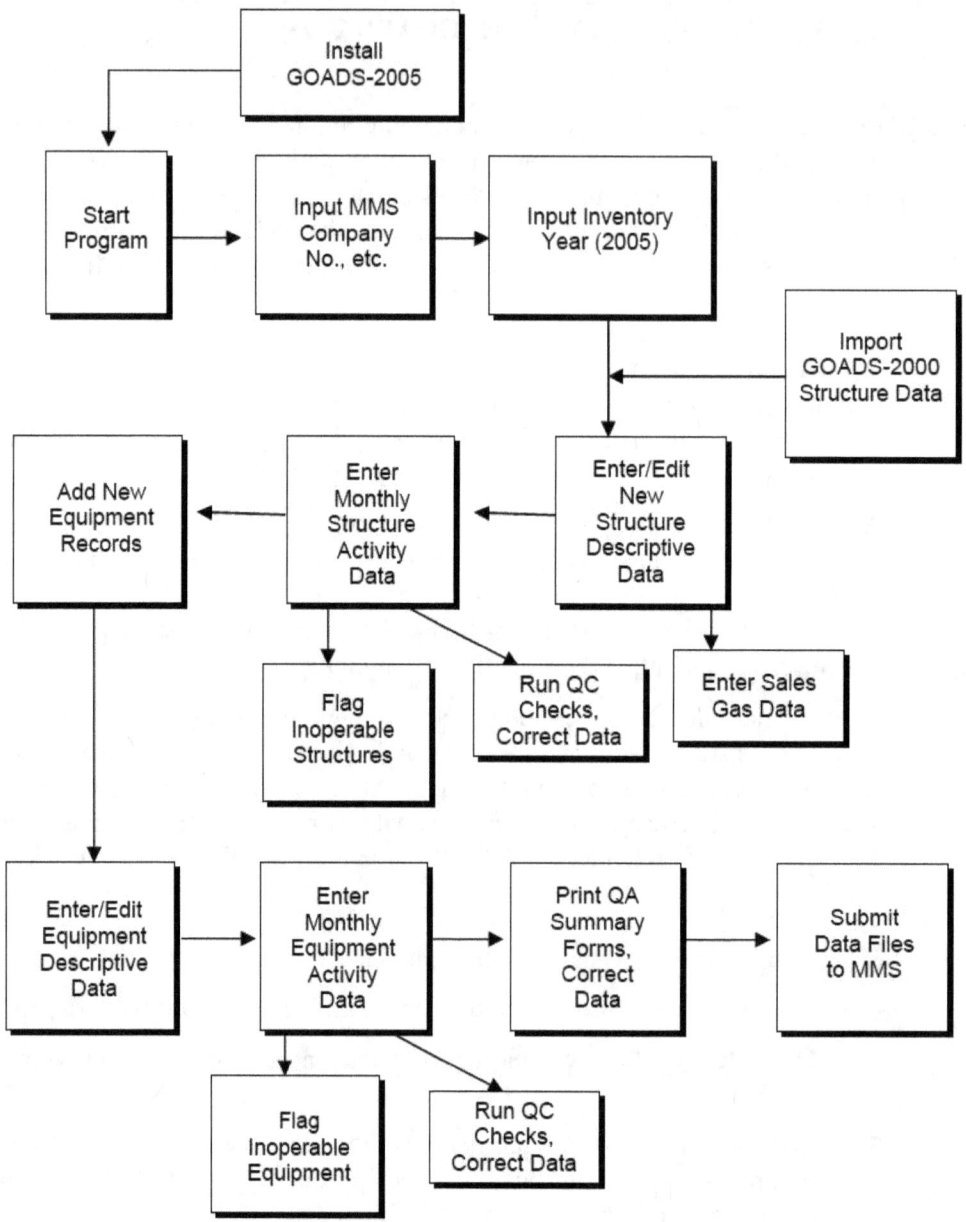

Figure 2-1. Populating GOADS-2005.

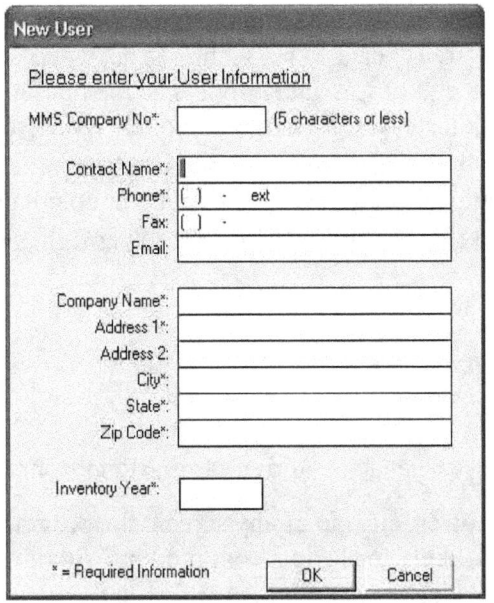

Figure 2-2. New User Screen.

The "New User" screen asks for "MMS Company No." It is extremely important that you use the correct MMS Company Number. It can be found in a separate document stored on the Installation CD. This ID cannot be changed once entered. The inventory year is 2005.

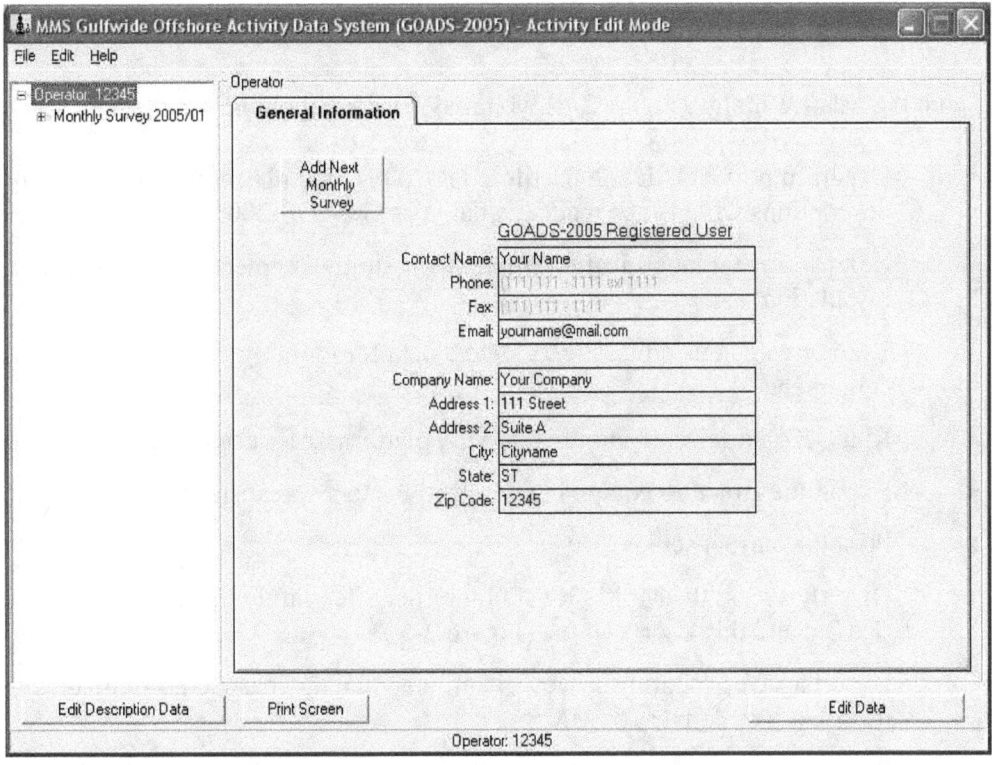

Figure 2-3. GOADS-2005 Main Window.

The GOADS-2005 program has a new feature that distinguishes between static (descriptive) and dynamic (activity) data. This feature is designed to reduce data entry time by requesting static platform and equipment data only once (as opposed to every month). The title bar at the top of the screen indicates the current edit mode. When you select Edit > Change to Description Edit Mode from the main menu, or Edit Description Data on the lower left side of any screen, the program allows you to enter/edit data that do not change from month to month. To edit the descriptive data, select Edit Data on the lower right side of any screen.

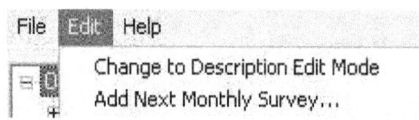

When you select Edit > Change to Activity Edit Mode from the main menu, or Edit Activity Data on the lower left side of any screen, the program allows you to enter/edit monthly activity data that are likely to change from month to month. In this mode you see the descriptive data, but it cannot be edited. Edit the activity data, select Edit Data on the lower right side of any screen.

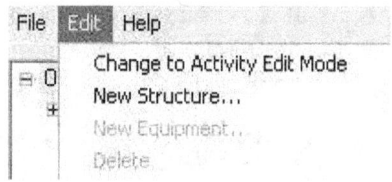

From the Main Window (Figure 2-4), you may perform the following tasks:

- Export/import GOADS-2005 files. GOADS-2000 platform and equipment descriptions will also be made available as GOADS-2005 Import files.

- Edit participant identification information (initially entered during program installation).

- View, create new, edit, save, or delete data for monthly surveys, facilities, or equipment.

- Run QC on a selected monthly survey, platform, of piece of equipment.

- Export the structure/equipment descriptions to a spreadsheet.

- Print the current screen.

- Directly access the MMS GOADS Internet Site with Frequently Asked Questions (FAQs) and this User's Guide (Figure 2-5).

- Export a saved monthly survey or entire annual database to a floppy disk or CD for backup or delivery to MMS.

- Print the QA Summary Form (must be printed when file is submitted to MMS; highlights key data that are missing) (see Section 3.3).

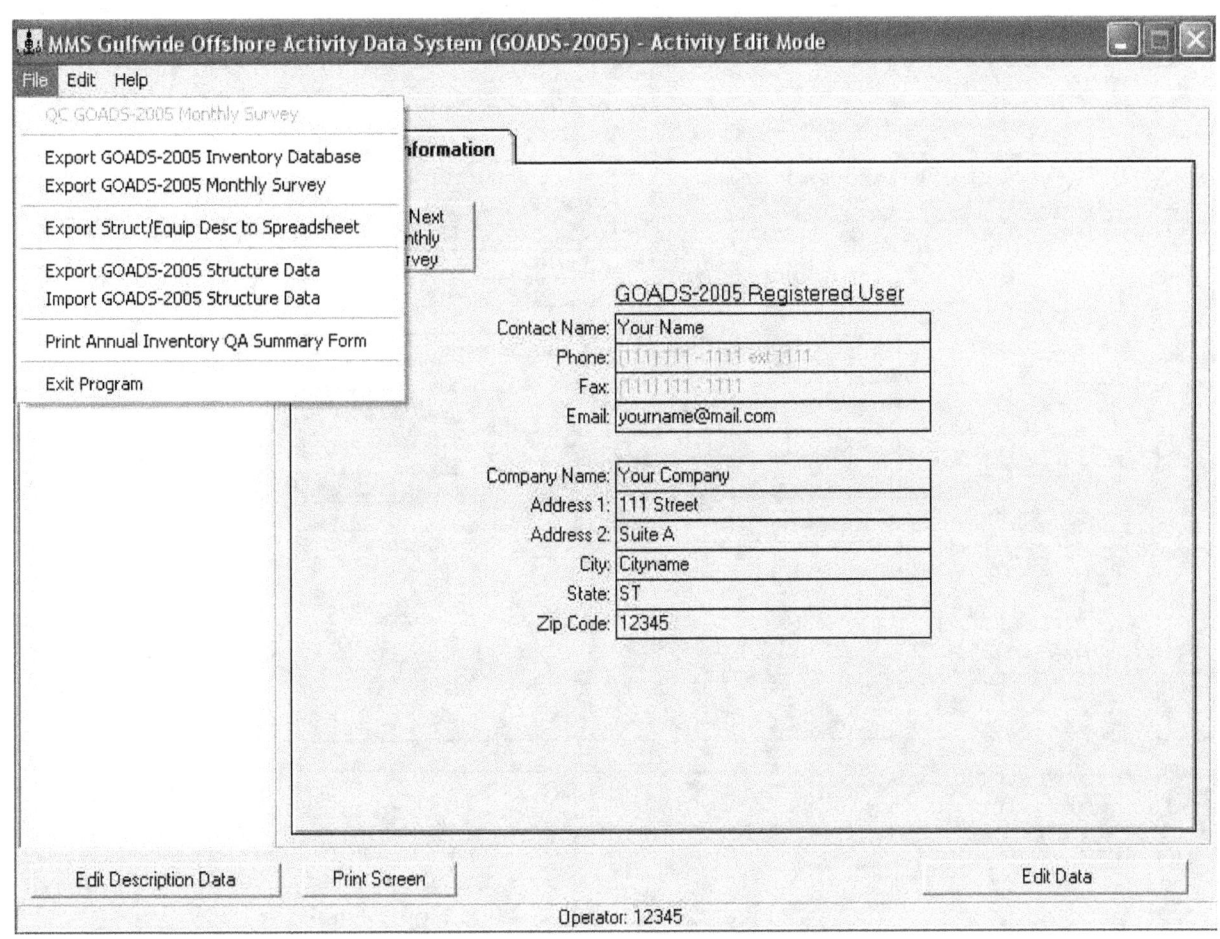

Figure 2-4. GOADS-2005 Main Menu.

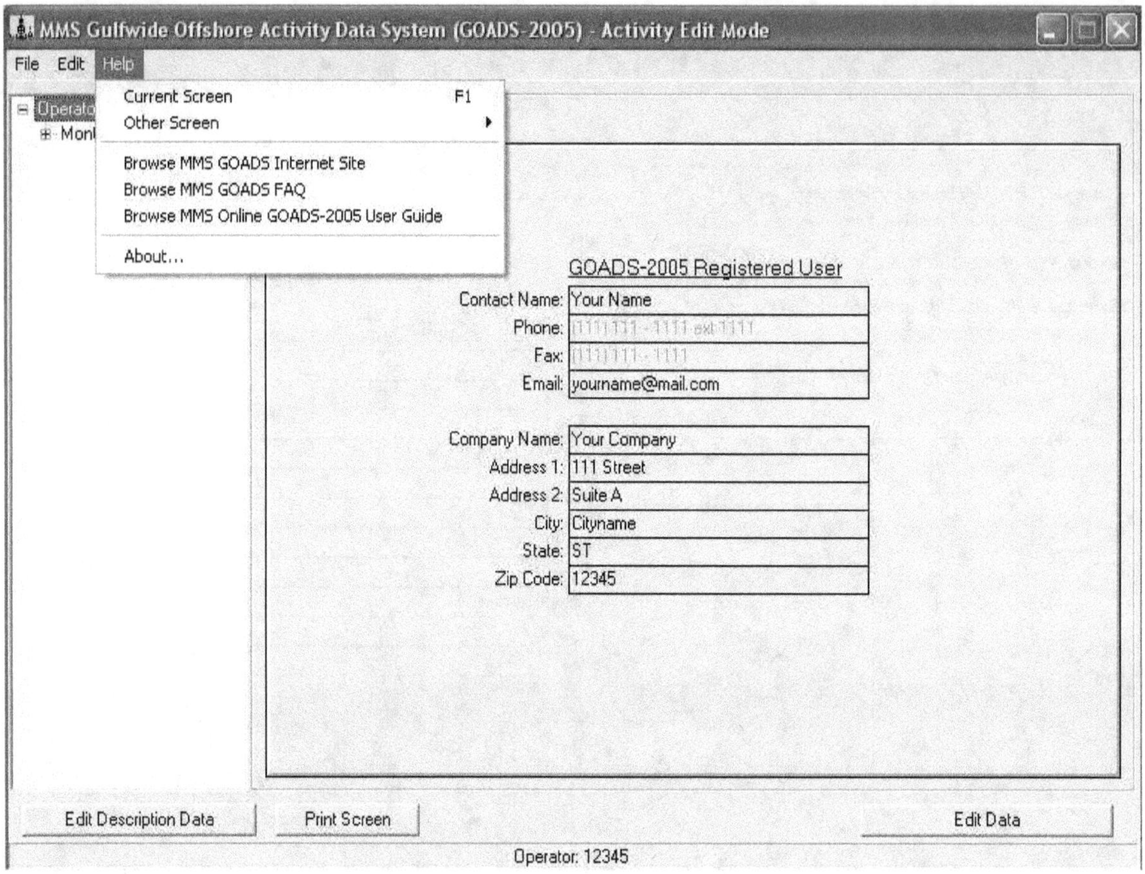

Figure 2-5. GOADS-2005 Help Menu.

Use one of the following ways to exit the program: (1) click **File | Exit Program** from the Main Window menu, or (2) click the ⊠ symbol at the upper right to close the program window. When you close the program window or select File | Exit Program from the main menu, a message box will appear asking if you would like to compact the database. As you add more data to GOADS-2005, we recommend that you say "YES" when prompted. Over time, the database can grow significantly, especially if you run the QA summary report multiple times.

If you have never used GOADS-2000, you can skip this section and go directly to Section 2.2 "Creating and Editing Data." If you have used GOADS-2000, you should read this section before proceeding.

If you were a GOADS-2000 user, you can import your GOADS-2000 platform and equipment <u>descriptive</u> data into GOADS-2005 before proceeding (described below). This platform and equipment descriptive data may be slightly different from your original submittal to MMS; it has undergone extensive QA/QC by MMS and may have been adjusted as a result. **You can and must edit the descriptive data after importing it to reflect any structural or equipment changes since 2000**.

GOADS-2005 has a new platform data import/export feature. The 2000 data are provided in this format so that they may be imported as if they had been exported in the same format.

To import the GOADS-2000 data, select File|Import GOADS-2005 Structure data. (Named as such because the 2000 data are in the GOADS-2005 required structure.) A dialog box will appear which lists any descriptive data that have been previously imported. The first time you import a file, this list will be blank. Enter the path and file name of the GOADS-2000 file you wish to import in the box labeled "Import File Path and Filename." You can also use the "Browse" button to find the file you wish to import (Figure 2-6). After you have selected a file, select Import Selected Structures . The GOADS-2000 file will be imported (this may take a few seconds) as January 2005. When the import process is complete, the survey name and its associated structures and equipment types should appear in the Navigation tree on the left of the screen. You must repeat this import process for all of your GOADS-2000 files (if you received multiple 2000 files).

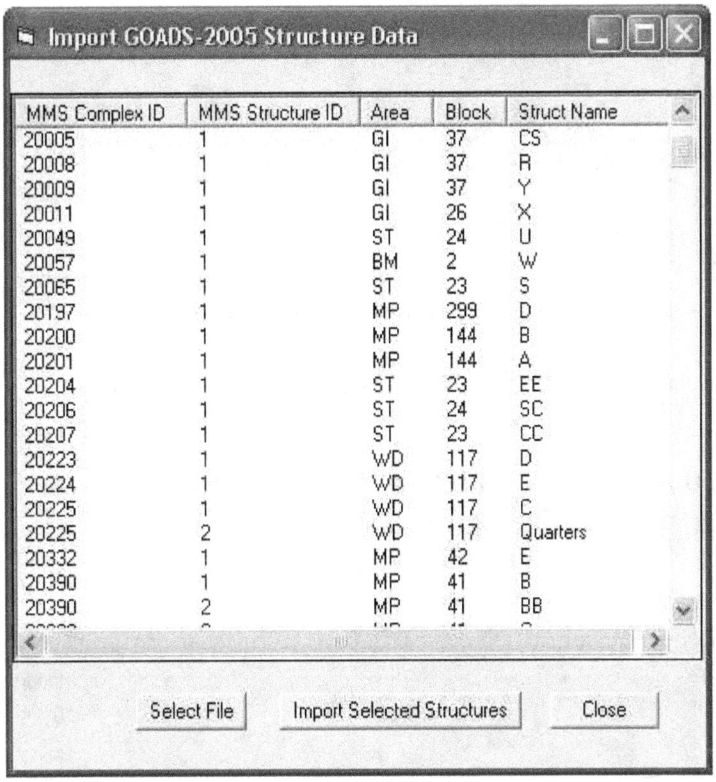

MMS Complex ID	MMS Structure ID	Area	Block	Struct Name
20005	1	GI	37	CS
20008	1	GI	37	R
20009	1	GI	37	Y
20011	1	GI	26	X
20049	1	ST	24	U
20057	1	BM	2	W
20065	1	ST	23	S
20197	1	MP	299	D
20200	1	MP	144	B
20201	1	MP	144	A
20204	1	ST	23	EE
20206	1	ST	24	SC
20207	1	ST	23	CC
20223	1	WD	117	D
20224	1	WD	117	E
20225	1	WD	117	C
20225	2	WD	117	Quarters
20332	1	MP	42	E
20390	1	MP	41	B
20390	2	MP	41	BB

Select File   Import Selected Structures   Close

Figure 2-6. GOADS-2005 Import Screen.

You can also use the File|Import GOADS-2005 Structure data feature to upload data for a structure that has been purchased in 2005 from another company. The User ID in the imported file will automatically be updated to your User ID. This process will import descriptive as well as monthly activity data, as available. The previous operator of that structure uses the corresponding File|Export GOADS-2005 Structure data to create this file (Figure 2-7).

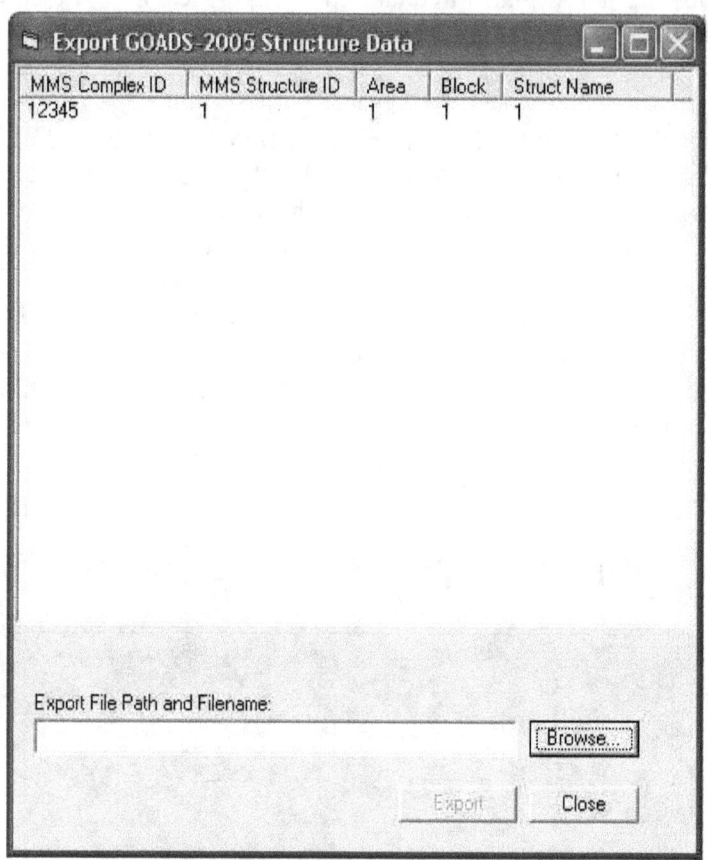

Figure 2-7. GOADS-2005 Export Screen.

2.2   CREATING AND EDITING DATA

2.2.1   Creating and Editing Structure Data

In order to create new structure data, from the Description Edit Mode, select Edit | New Structure from the Main Window menu.

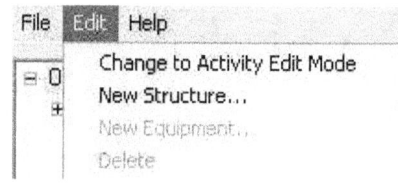

A New Structure Dialog Box will appear to request vital identification data for the structure (Figure 2-8). See Appendix A for guidance on entering these data correctly.

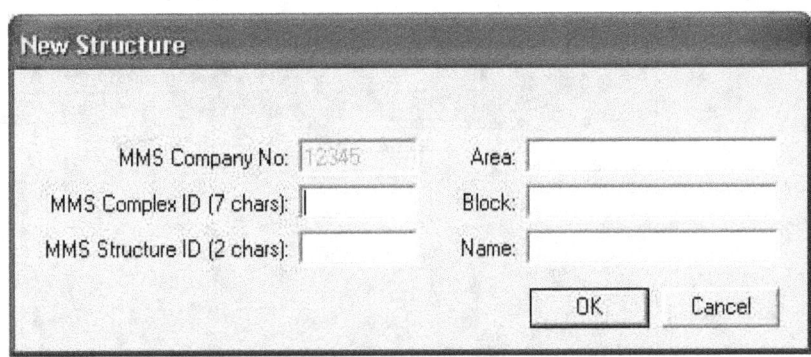

Figure 2-8. New Structure Dialog Box.

Enter the information and click OK . An icon for the new structure will appear in the Navigation Tree on the left side of the Main Window. Highlight the new structure icon to view the Structure Screen.

Figures 2-9 and 2-10 show the Structure screen in Description Edit Mode and Activity Edit Mode.

In the Description Edit Mode, the Structure Screen contains three tabs: *General Information, Sales Gas,* and *QC Results*. *General Information* shows contact and other general information for the current structure. Note that production is the quantity of petroleum that was extracted from the ground *at the structure*; throughput is the total quantity of petroleum handled at the structure, including petroleum extracted at another location and transferred to the structure. *Sales Gas* presents the volumetric composition of the natural gas processed at the structure and transferred off the structure (Figure 2-11). *QC Results* tabulates any quality control errors that may be encountered as data are completed for the current structure and its associated equipment (see Section 2.3). In the Activity Edit Mode, the *Sales Gas* tab is not visible because it contains data that do not change from month to month.

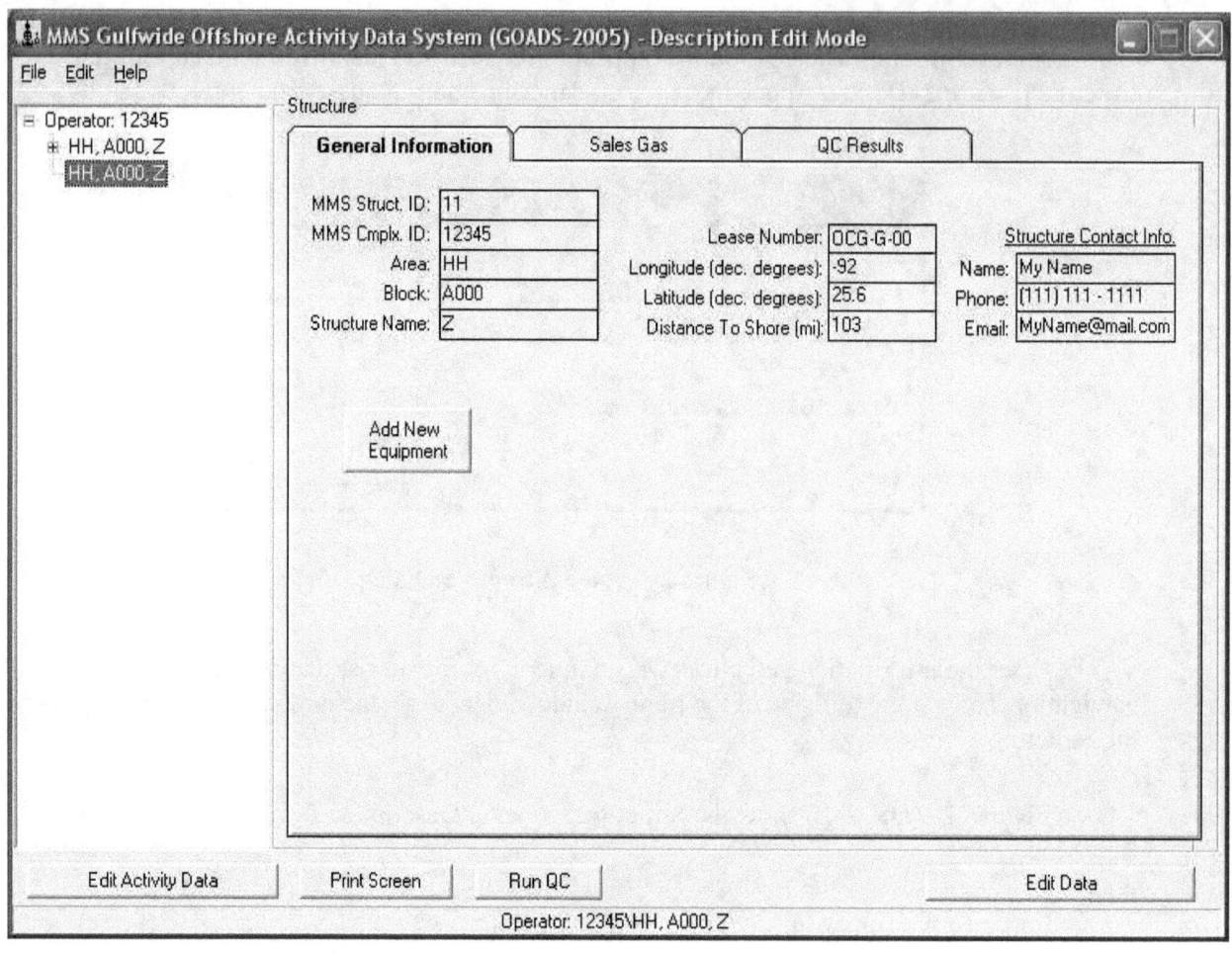

Figure 2-9. Structure Screen in Description Edit Mode.

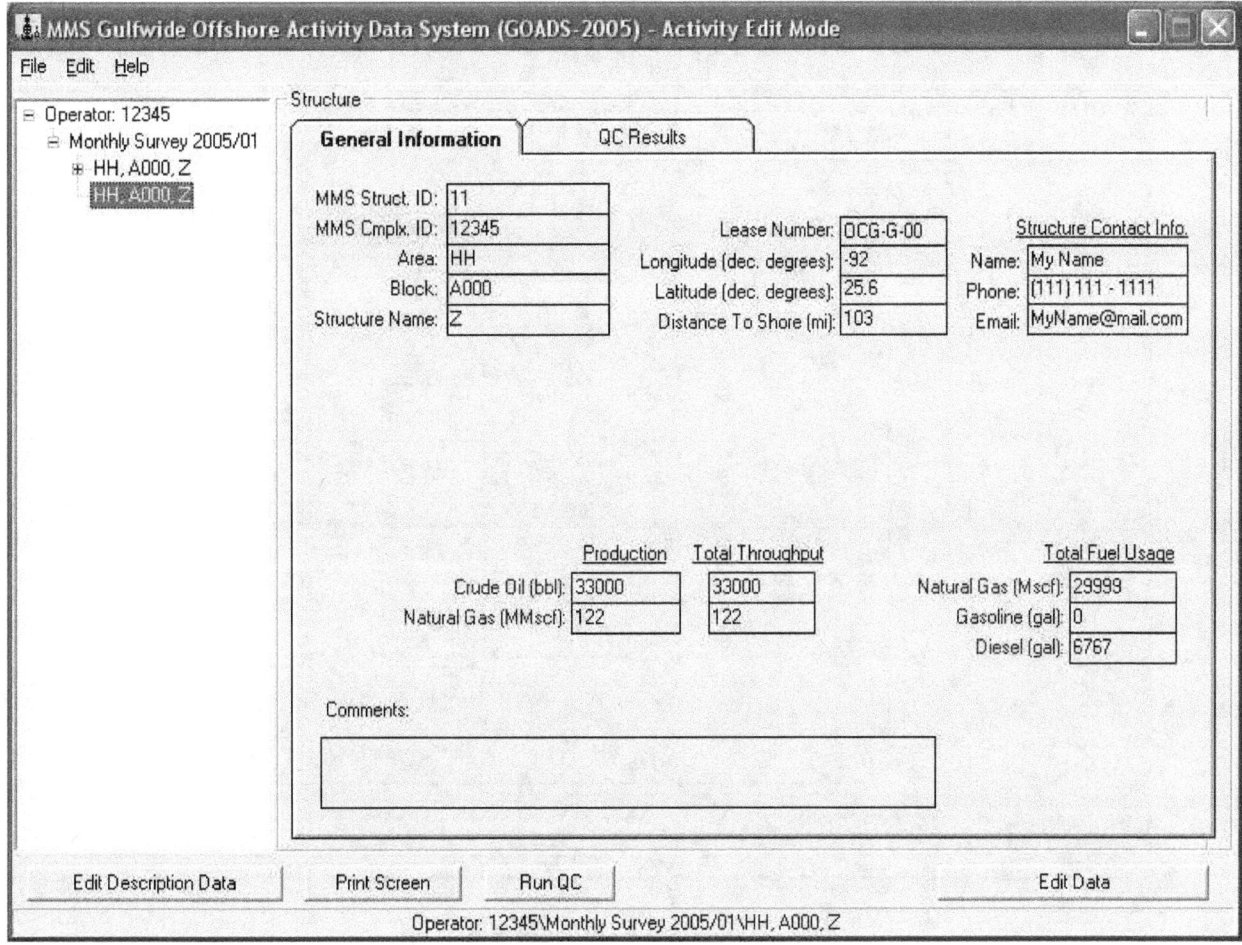

Figure 2-10. Structure Screen in Activity Edit Mode.

The following buttons are available on the Structure Screen from either the Description Edit Mode or the Activity Edit Mode:

- Edit Data launches Edit Mode so that changes or new data may be entered.

- Run QC runs quality control checks on all data saved for the current structure and its associated equipment.

- Print Screen to print the current screen for review.

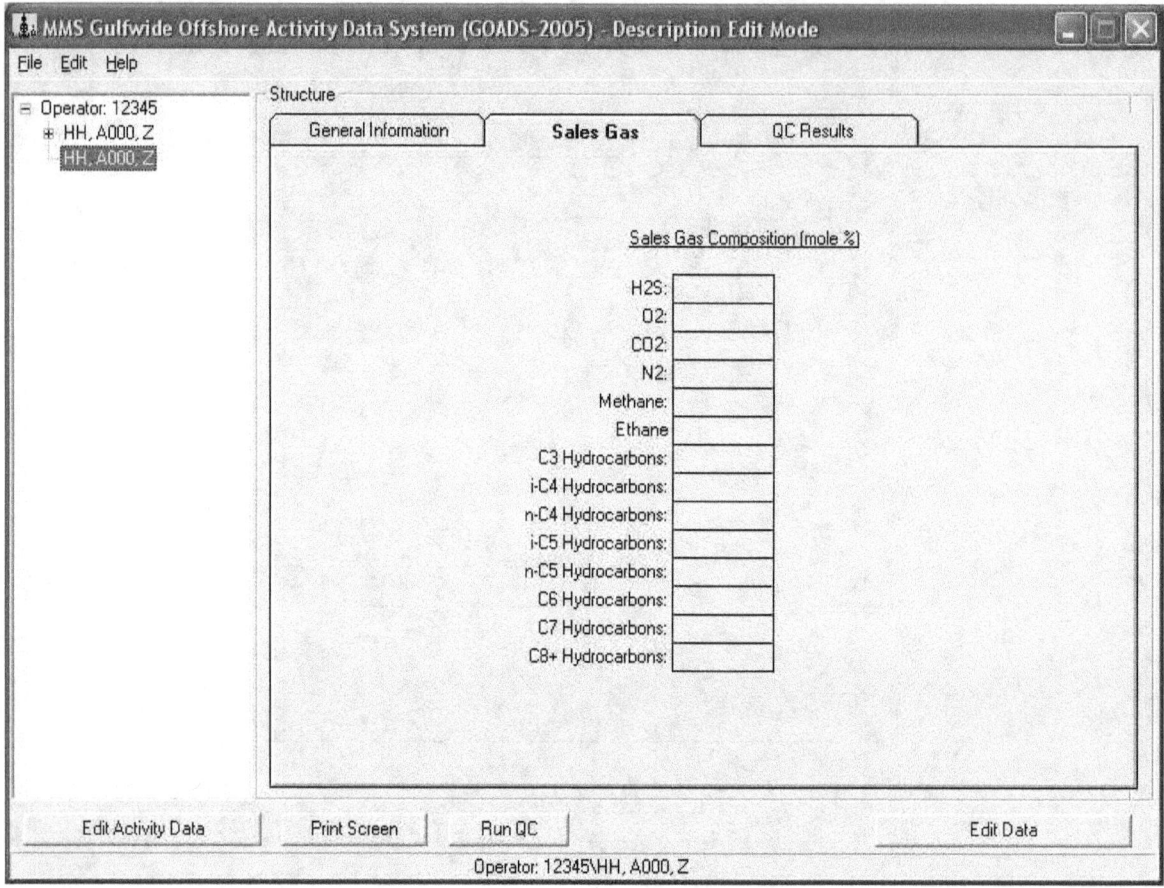

Figure 2-11. Sales Gas Screen.

Four additional buttons become available in the Activity Edit Mode:

- $\boxed{\text{Save}}$ (only available in Edit Mode) incrementally saves work and returns to Edit Mode.

- $\boxed{\text{Cancel}}$ (only available in Edit Mode) discard recent changes and close Edit Mode.

- $\boxed{\text{End Edit \& Save}}$ (only available in Edit Mode) saves changes and exits Edit Mode.

- $\boxed{\text{No Emissions to Report}}$ to flag a structure as inactive for a given month.

From the Activity Edit Mode, new monthly surveys can be created. An icon for the new survey will appear in the Navigation Tree on the left side of the Main Window. Previously entered equipment descriptive data (see Section 2.2.2) will automatically be copied into the new monthly survey. Highlight the survey icon to view the Survey Screen. The Survey Screen contains only one tab: *QC Results*. *QC Results* tabulates any quality control errors encountered during data entry (see Section 2.3).

2.2.2 Creating and Editing Equipment Data

GOADS-2005 queries for information regarding the following sources of emissions:

- Amine gas sweetening unit
- Boiler/heater/burner
- Drilling rig
- Combustion flare
- Fugitive losses
- Gasoline/diesel engine
- Glycol dehydrator
- Loading operation
- Losses from flashing
- Mud degassing
- Natural gas engine
- Natural gas turbine
- Pneumatic pumps
- Pressure/level controllers
- Storage tank
- Cold vent

In order to create new equipment data, go to the Navigation Tree on the left side of the Main Window and select the appropriate structure (into which the new equipment data will be placed). Select **Edit | New Equipment** from the Main Window menu.

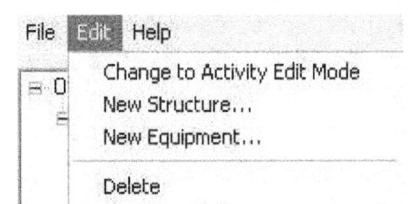

A New Equipment Dialog Box will request vital identification data for the equipment, such as equipment ID number and equipment type (e.g., flares, turbines, etc.) (Figure 2-12). Enter the information, then click $\boxed{\text{OK}}$. An icon for the new equipment will appear in the Navigation Tree on the left side of the Main Window and a new screen will automatically open, specific to the equipment type entered. You can return to this equipment screen at any time by highlighting the equipment.

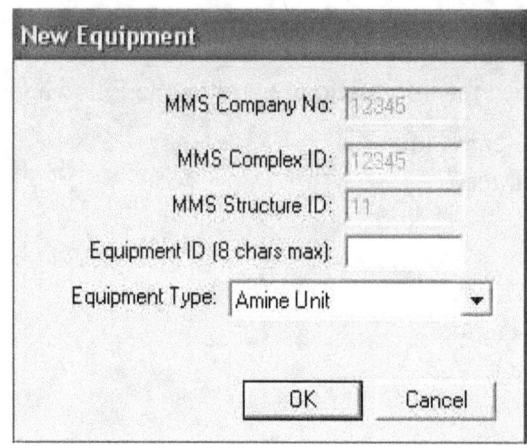

Figure 2-12. New Equipment Dialog Box.

Depending on the equipment type and the edit mode, the equipment screen will contain two to four tabs: *General Information, Exhaust/Ventilation System, Control Equipment,* and *QC Results. General Information* shows operating parameters for the current equipment. From the Description Edit Mode, you can populate/edit static equipment description data that do not change from month to month. When you create a new monthly survey, these data are automatically copied. From the Activity Edit Mode, you are prompted to enter activity data that can vary from month to month. These data are not copied automatically when a new monthly survey is created.

Exhaust/Ventilation System presents variables that are related to equipment exhaust systems; this screen is not visible when you are in Activity Edit Mode. *Control Equipment* permits users to describe installed pollution control devices that were not accounted for on the *General Information* tab; this screen is also not visible when you are in Activity Edit Mode. *QC Results* tabulates any quality control errors that may be encountered as data are completed for the equipment (see Section 2.3).

In Edit Activity Data you can select No Emissions to Report for a given month for the entire platform or specific pieces of equipment. This is an important new feature; MMS will assume that the platform or equipment are NOT operating for months flagged as such, regardless of other values that may be populated for the month. The user does not have to fill in the forms with zeros for inactive structures or equipment, merely check this box. Records flagged as no emissions to report will not be QC checked in the inventory development process.

If you do NOT select ⬛No Emissions to Report⬛ MMS will assume that the platform or equipment is operating that month, and surrogate data will be used to develop emission estimates if necessary.

MMS will also assume that activity values that are left blank (Null) should be populated with surrogate data.

The following buttons are available on the Description Edit Mode and Activity Edit Mode Equipment Screens: Activity values that are populated with zeros will NOT be populated with surrogate data.

- ⬛Edit Data⬛ launches Edit Mode so that changes or new data may be entered.
- ⬛Run QC⬛ runs quality control checks on data for the current equipment.
- ⬛Print Screen⬛ to print the current screen for review

Four additional buttons become available only in Activity Edit Mode:

- ⬛Save⬛ (only available in Edit Mode) incrementally saves work and returns to Edit Mode.
- ⬛No Emissions to Report⬛ to flag equipment as inactive for a given month.
- ⬛Cancel⬛ (only available in Edit Mode) discard recent changes and close Edit Mode.
- ⬛End Edit & Save⬛ (only available in Edit Mode) saves changes and exits Edit Mode.

2.3   QUALITY CONTROL TESTS

After you complete and save data, GOADS-2005 automatically runs a series of quality control (QC) checks before saving the data. If any entries are incomplete, atypical, or suspect, a pop-up message will appear, and a list of QC errors will appear on the *QC Results* tab (Figure 2-13). You may choose to return and correct the problems, to override QC check(s) (a comment is required), or to ignore message(s) and save changes anyway. If QC problems remain uncorrected and uncommented when the data are submitted, MMS staff members will attempt to reconcile missing, atypical, or suspect data by reviewing the comments or contacting you by telephone.

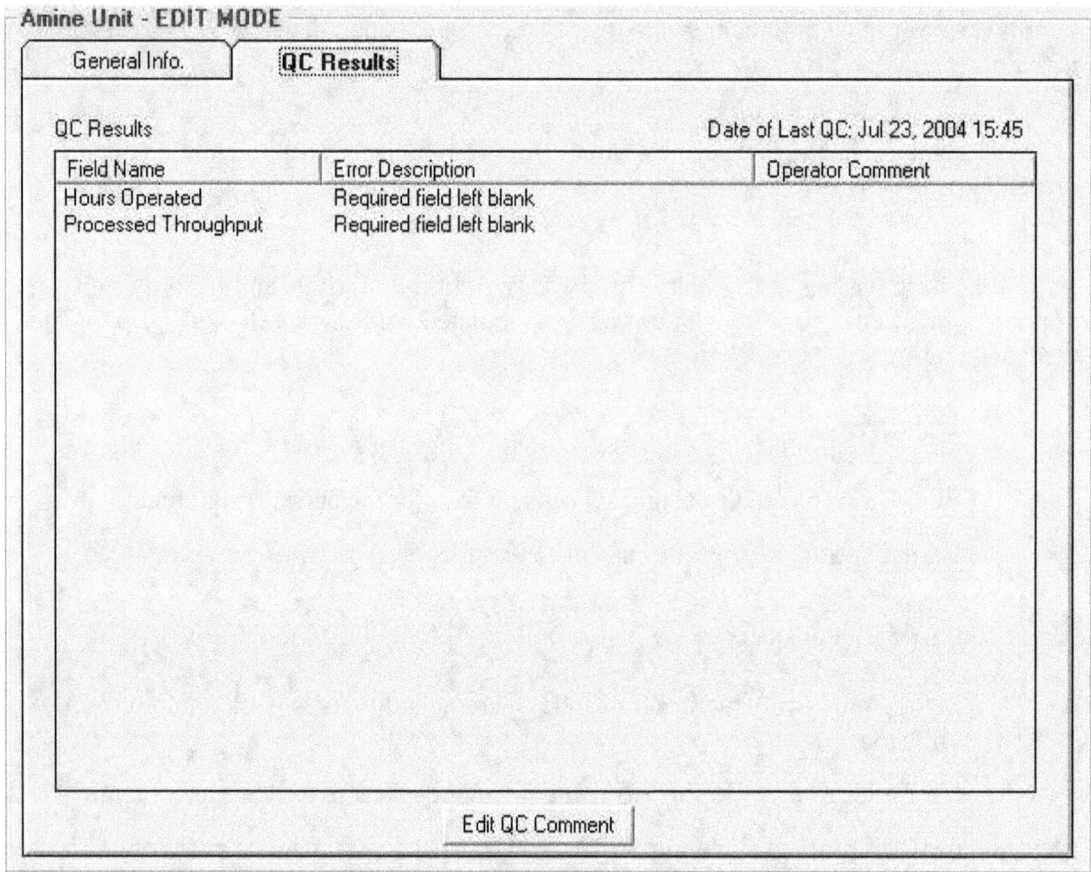

Figure 2-13. QC Results Tab.

2.4 SAVING AND BACKING UP WORK

It is very important to periodically store data to a secure location other than the hard drive (such as a floppy disk or CD). This practice minimizes data loss in the event of a computer failure or other mishap.

After you complete and save data, the entries are saved to a working file on the hard drive[1]. (In order to discard changes, click Cancel instead of End Edit & Save.) In order to store data in an alternate location, select File|Export GOADS-2005 Inventory Database on the main menu. A dialog box will appear which will allow you to enter a File Path and Filename or browse to the location in which you wish to create the file. After entering the path and file name, hit "OK." You can then copy the file you have created to CD, floppy disk or zip disk.

---

[1] The working file is located at C:\Program Files\GOADS-2005\GOADS.mdb. The working file should be backed up periodically by copying to a secure location.

2.5   SETTING STATUS OF FACILITIES AND EQUIPMENT

If equipment or an entire structure becomes inactive for an _entire_ monthly survey period, the change in status should be noted by selecting `No Emissions to Report` but only for the affected survey period(s). Note that when a piece of equipment or a structure is active for any part of a survey period, its status should NOT be set to No Emissions To Report.

Open an affected survey in the Navigation Tree on the left side of the Main Window. (Double-click the survey icon, or click the `+` symbol immediately to its left.) Select the affected structure or equipment, and click `Edit Data` in order to launch Edit Mode. Use the Set Status data entry boxes to change the status. Indicate the new status and its effective date and click `End Edit & Save` in order to record the change in status.

2.6   FINDING HELP AND EXTRA INFORMATION

Each screen has an associated help text file that contains technical details about the required data entries, such as definitions, quality control checks, typical values, estimation methods, etc. Access help by pressing the `F1` key. You can also go to the Help menu and select "current screen" to view the help file for the current screen or select "other screen" and see a list of all available help files. Help files are reprinted in Appendix A of this User's Guide. In addition, you can directly access the MMS GOADS Internet Site with Frequently Asked Questions (FAQs) and this User's Guide from within GOADS-2005.

The main GOADS-2005 webpage is at:

www.gomr.mms.gov/homepg/regulate/environ/airquality/goad.html

For information on how to resolve technical problems or other difficulties, go to:

www.gomr.mms.gov/homepg/regulate/environ/airquality/faqgoad.html

3. UPON SURVEY COMPLETION

3.1 HOW, WHEN, AND WHERE TO DELIVER DATA FILES

When the entire inventory is completed (12 monthly surveys), it should be exported to your hard-drive and then copied to CD, zip disk, or floppy disk for submittal to MMS.

To export the inventory, select **File|Export GOADS-2005 Inventory Database** on the main menu. A dialog box will appear which will allow you to enter a File Path and Filename or browse to the location in which you wish to create the file. After entering the path and file name, click "OK." You can then copy the file you have created to the appropriate medium.

The MMS should receive all 2005 data files before April 21, 2006. Floppies or CDs should be placed in cardboard mailing envelopes and mailed to the address below.

> Ms. Holli Ensz
> Minerals Management Service
> Office of Leasing and Environment (MS 5433)
> 1201 Elmwood Park Blvd.
> New Orleans, LA 70123-2394
> Phone: (504) 736-2536
> E-Mail: holli.ensz@mms.gov

3.2 FAILED QUALITY CONTROL TESTS

When saving data to the floppy drive or CD for delivery to MMS, GOADS-2005 stores the results of all QC tests. If the user returns to GOADS-2005 in order to address QC problems, the error messages may be reviewed from the *QC Results* tab on the Survey Screen. If you choose to ignore errors and submit the data anyway, MMS staff members will attempt to reconcile the problems by reviewing comments or contacting you by telephone.

3.3 QA SUMMARY FORM

From the Main Window (Figure 2-4), the **File | Print Annual Inventory QA Summary Form** may be selected at any time to view and obtain a hard-copy printout of key missing and inconsistent data elements (Figure 3-1). These data elements are critical if MMS is to develop emission estimates for the equipment listed.

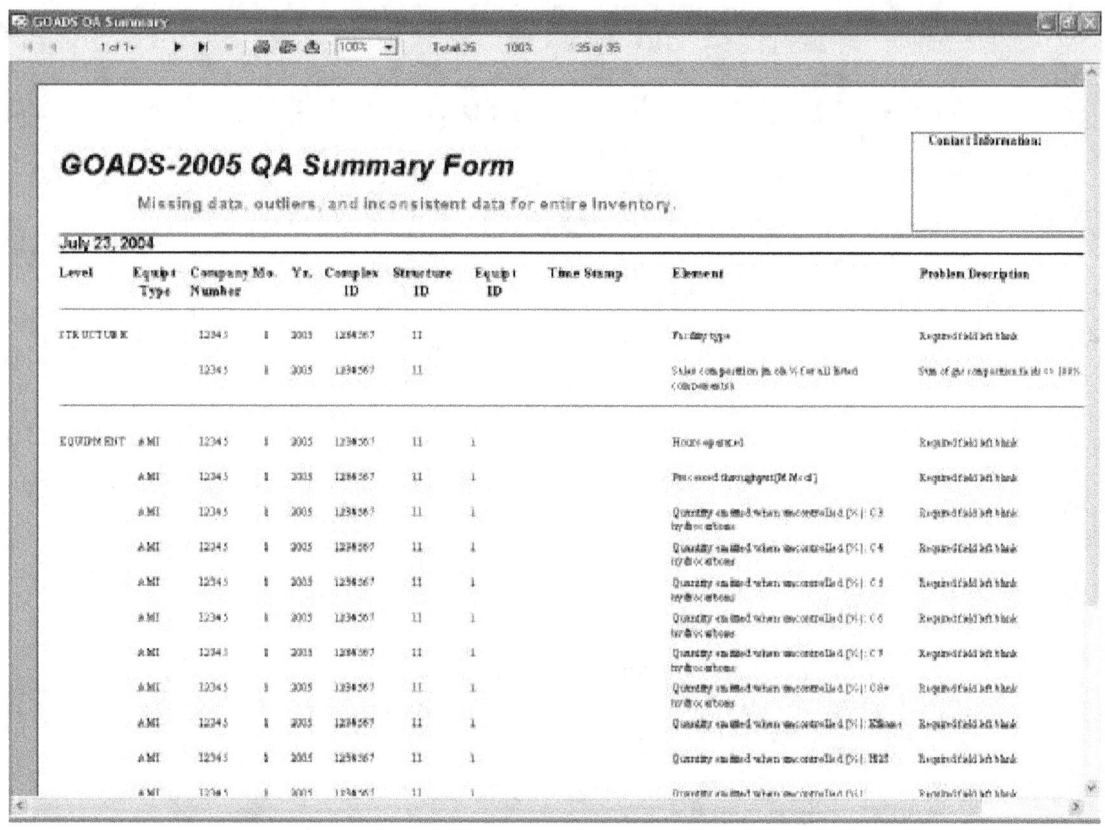

Figure 3-1. QA Summary Form Screen.

In addition, a hard-copy printout of the QA Summary Form must be submitted along with your data files to facilitate review by MMS staff members. The data files may be directly returned to you if the QA Summary Form indicates missing or inconsistent key data elements. Appendix B presents the key data elements in the QA Summary Form.

APPENDIX A

HELP TEXT FILES

A.1   USER INFORMATION

A.1.1   General Information Tab

GOADS-2005 Registered User – Identifies the person to whom GOADS-2005 is registered, an employee of the company that owns structures in the outer continental shelf. This should be the primary contact person who is responsible for submitting surveys to the MMS. The following contact information should be provided:

- Name
- Phone number
- Fax number
- Email address (optional)
- Company name
- Street address
- City
- State
- Zip code

A.2   STRUCTURE INFORMATION

A.2.1   General Information Tab

MMS Structure ID - A unique identifier code that is assigned to an offshore structure prior to its construction by the MMS. This identifier code is tracked in the Minerals Management Service's records.

MMS Complex ID - A unique identifier code that is assigned to a group of related structures prior to construction by the MMS. This identifier code is tracked in the Minerals Management Service's records.

Area Name – Designated name of the geographic area in which the structure is located.

Block Number – Designated number of the geographical block in which the structure is located.

Name - A name or identifier that denotes a structure within its Area/Block.

Lease Number - The lease number issued by the Minerals Management Service for the construction and operation of an offshore structure.

Longitude (decimal degrees) – An east-west coordinate that defines the position of an offshore structure. Specify to at least four decimal places.

Latitude (decimal degrees) – An north-south coordinate that defines the position of an offshore structure. Specify to at least four decimal places.

Distance to shore (miles) - The distance to the nearest U.S. shoreline. Specify to the nearest 1/10 mile.

Structure contact information - The name, phone number, and/or email address of an individual who may be contacted with questions regarding the survey data, such as the structure's supervising engineer.

Production - Describes the natural gas or oil products that were extracted at this structure during the specific survey period.

- Crude Oil Production (barrels): The quantity of crude oil extracted at this structure.

- Natural Gas Production (million standard cubic feet): The quantity of natural gas extracted at this structure, volume adjusted to standard temperature and pressure (60 degrees Fahrenheit, 1 atmosphere).

Throughput - The total volume of natural gas or oil products handled at the current structure during the survey period, including production volumes and volumes transferred via pipeline from another location.

- Crude Oil Throughput (barrels): The total quantity of crude oil handled at the current structure.

- Natural Gas Throughput (million standard cubic feet): The total quantity of natural gas handled at the current structure, volume adjusted to standard temperature and pressure (60 degrees Fahrenheit, 1 atmosphere).

Total fuel usage - The quantity of fuel consumed at this structure during the specific survey period.

- Natural gas fuel usage (thousand standard cubic feet) - The quantity of natural gas consumed at this structure.

- Gasoline usage (gallons) - The quantity of gasoline consumed at this structure.

- Diesel fuel usage (gallons) - The quantity of diesel fuel consumed at this structure.

No Emissions to Report - Indicates the status of the structure for the specific survey period.

"No Emissions to Report" - Indicates that the structure and all of its equipment were unused for the entire month-long survey period. The Enter Edit Mode button will be disabled for all equipment belonging to the structure, and all equipment will be treated as inactive.

Comments - A space for general user comments regarding this structure, with a maximum length of 255 characters.

A.2.2 Sales Gas Data

Sales Composition (mole percent) – The volumetric composition (percent by volume = mole percent) of the natural gas processed at the structure and transferred off the structure. If a constituent is not present, enter 0. The composition should sum to 100%.

A.2.3 QC Results Tab

Error Source – List of input variables, structures, and/or equipment for this survey that have been flagged with QC error messages.

Error Description – List of the reasons that QC error messages were assigned.

Operator Comment – List of user's explanations for unusual or unexpected values that were flagged with QC error messages. An operator comment indicates that the user wishes to override the QC error message. (Select an error message, then click "Add QC Comment" in order to add Operator Comments.)

A.3   AMINE GAS SWEETENING UNIT

A.3.1   General Information Tab

Processed throughput (million standard cubic feet) – The total volume of natural gas processed by this amine unit during the specific monthly survey period, volume adjusted to standard temperature and pressure (60 degrees Fahrenheit, 1 atmosphere).

Hours operated – The total number of hours that this amine unit was in operation during the specific monthly survey period.

Amine unit elevation (feet above mean sea level) – The elevation of the amine unit at its base above mean sea level.

Unprocessed natural gas concentrations (percent by volume) – The volumetric concentrations of constituents present in the unprocessed natural gas stream, including the following:

- Hydrogen Sulfide
- Methane (CH_4)
- Ethane (C_2H_6)
- C3 Hydrocarbons (hydrocarbons with 3 carbon atoms in their molecular structure)
- C4 Hydrocarbons
- C5 Hydrocarbons
- C6 Hydrocarbons
- C7 Hydrocarbons
- C8+ Hydrocarbons (hydrocarbons with 8 or more carbon atoms in their molecular structure)

Specify emissions by model inputs or quantity emitted when uncontrolled (%) - Select model inputs if you do not have information on the uncontrolled quantity emitted. Proceed to the model inputs screen if the data are not available.

Quantity emitted when uncontrolled (percent) – The mass percent emitted to the atmosphere of each constituent in the unprocessed natural gas stream, without accounting for any installed control equipment. Specify to the nearest 1/100 percent, if possible. If the data are not readily available, it is not mandatory that you enter this data.

A.3.2   Model Inputs Tab

Amine type – Indicates the type of amine used in this unit, monoethanolamine (MEA), diethanolamine (DEA), tertiaryethanolamine (TEA), methyldiethanolamine (MDEA), diglycolamine (DGA).

Unprocessed sour gas feed pressure (pounds per square inch gauge) – The pressure of the unprocessed sour gas feed.

Unprocessed sour gas feed temperature (degrees Fahrenheit) – The temperature of the unprocessed sour gas feed.

Equipped with a flash tank? (yes/no) – Indicates whether the system is equipped with a flash tank.

Flash tank temperature (degrees Fahrenheit) – The temperature of the flash tank.

Flash tank pressure (pounds per square inch gauge) – The pressure of the flash tank.

Destination of flash gas – Indicates if the gas is vented to the atmosphere, routed to a separator, recycled to an absorber, or burned in a flare.

Number of absorber trays – Indicates the number of absorber trays on this amine unit.

Lean amine feed pressure (pounds per square inch gauge) – The pressure of the lean amine feed.

Lean amine feed temperature (degrees Fahrenheit) – The temperature of the lean amine feed.

Lean amine volumetric flowrate (gallons per minute) – The rate of amine circulation through the unit.

Lean amine feed amine content (percent by weight) – The amine content of the lean amine feed.

Lean amine feed H_2S concentration (percent by volume) – The volumetric concentration of H_2S present in the lean amine feed.

Lean amine feed CO_2 concentration (percent by volume) – The volumetric concentration of CO_2 present in the lean amine feed.

No Emissions to Report – Indicates the status of the amine unit for the specific survey period.

- "No Emissions to Report" - Indicates that the equipment was unused for the entire month-long survey period.

Comments - A space for general user comments regarding this structure, with a maximum length of 255 characters.

A.3.3   Ventilation System Tab for Acid Gas from the Reboiler

Emissions destination – Indicates whether the emissions from this equipment are vented or flared locally, or at some distance from the equipment.

Low-pressure vent/flare ID – Indicates the destination vent or flare identifier code (if emissions are not vented or flared locally). It may be necessary to first create a vent or flare before it will appear in the list (using the Edit|New Equipment menu).

Outlet height (feet above mean sea level) – The elevation of the stack outlet above mean sea level.

Outlet inner diameter (inches) – The effective diameter of a process vent/flare.

Exit velocity (feet/second) – The exit velocity of emissions through the outlet of a process vent/flare.

Exit temperature (degrees Fahrenheit) – The temperature of gaseous emissions measured at the outlet of a process vent.

Outlet orientation (degrees) – The deviation of the outlet from vertically upward. 0 indicates an upward pointing outlet; 180 indicates a downward pointing outlet.

Flare feed rate (standard cubic feet per hour) – The volumetric feed rate to a process flare.

Combustion temperature (degrees Fahrenheit) – The combustion temperature of a process flare.

Combustion efficiency (percent) – The combustion efficiency of a process flare, or the completeness of hydrocarbon conversion to carbon dioxide (as CO_2).

Installed control equipment – Indicates which common types of control devices are installed for this equipment.

Condenser temperature (degrees Fahrenheit) – The operating temperature of a condenser installed as a control device.

Condenser pressure (absolute pounds per square inch) – The operating pressure of a condenser installed as a control device.

Sulfur recovery efficiency (percent) – The efficiency for a sulfur recovery unit that is installed as a control device (as a percent of total sulfur).

A.3.4   Control Equipment Tab

Other control device? (yes/no) – Indicates whether additional controls are installed, other than the common control devices listed on the Ventilation System Tab.

Description – If present, a description of other control devices is required (other than those listed on the Ventilation System Tab).

SO_x efficiency (percent) – The total combined reductions in sulfur oxides emissions achieved by all other installed control devices (other than those listed on the Ventilation System Tab).

NO_x efficiency (percent) – The total combined reductions in nitrogen oxides emissions achieved by all other installed control devices (other than those listed on the Ventilation System Tab).

CO efficiency (percent) – The total combined reductions in carbon monoxide emissions achieved by all other installed control devices (other than those listed on the Ventilation System Tab).

VOC efficiency (percent) – The total combined reductions in volatile organics emissions achieved by all other installed control devices (other than those listed on the Ventilation System Tab).

PM_{10} efficiency (percent) – The total combined reductions in PM_{10} emissions (particulate matter under 10 microns in diameter) achieved by all other installed control devices (other than those listed on the Ventilation System Tab).

A.3.5 QC Results Tab

Error Source – List of input variables for this equipment that have been flagged with QC error messages.

Error Description – List of the reasons that QC error messages were assigned.

Operator Comment – List of user's explanations for unusual or unexpected values that were flagged with QC error messages. An operator comment indicates that the user wishes to override the QC error message. (Select an error message, then click "Add QC Comment" in order to add Operator Comments.)

A.4   BOILER/HEATER/BURNER

A.4.1   General Information Tab

Equipment elevation (feet above mean sea level) – The elevation of a boiler/heater/burner, measured from mean sea level to its base.

Hours operated – The total number of hours that this boiler/heater/burner was in operation during the specific monthly survey period.

Fuel type – The type of fuel burned by the equipment.

Fuel H_2S content (parts per million by volume) – The concentration of hydrogen sulfide in gaseous fuel types.

Fuel sulfur content (percent by mass) – The sulfur content in liquid fuel types.

Fuel heating value (British thermal units/standard cubic feet) – The energy content of gaseous fuel types.

Fuel heating value (British thermal units per pound) – The energy content of liquid fuel types.

Max rated heat input (million British thermal units per hour) – The manufacturer's maximum rated heat input rate.

Average heat input (million British thermal units per hour) – The average heat input rate during operation this survey period.

Max rated fuel usage (standard cubic feet per hour) – The maximum rate of gaseous fuel usage, volume adjusted to standard temperature and pressure (60 degrees Fahrenheit, 1 atmosphere).

Average fuel usage (standard cubic feet per hour) – The average rate of gaseous fuel usage during operation this survey period, volume adjusted to standard temperature and pressure (60 degrees Fahrenheit, 1 atmosphere).

Max rated fuel usage (pounds per hour) – The maximum rate of liquid fuel usage.

Average fuel usage (pounds per hour) – The average rate of liquid fuel usage during operation this survey period.

Total fuel used (thousand standard cubic feet) – Total gaseous fuel used during this survey period, volume adjusted to standard temperature and pressure (60 degrees Fahrenheit, 1 atmosphere). If you do not monitor actual fuel use for a boiler, heater, or burner, a value may be calculated using:

[Hours operated * average heat input (MMBtu/hr) * (10^6 Btu/MMBtu)]÷[fuel heating value (1,050 Btu/scf) * (1,000 scf/Mscf)].

A-10

Total fuel used (pounds) – Total liquid fuel used during this survey period. If you do not monitor actual fuel use for a boiler, heater, or burner, a value may be calculated using:

[Hours operated * average heat input (MMBtu/hr) * (10^6 Btu/MMBtu)]÷[fuel heating value (19,300 Btu/1b].

Note that the fuel heating value shown above is for diesel fuel.

No Emissions to Report – Indicates the status of the boiler/heater/burner for the specific survey period.

- "No Emissions to Report" – Indicates that the equipment was unused for the entire month-long survey period.

Comments – A space for general user comments regarding this structure, with a maximum length of 255 characters.

A.4.2   Exhaust System Tab

Outlet height (feet above mean sea level) – The elevation of the stack outlet above mean sea level.

Outlet inner diameter (inches) – The inner diameter of the exhaust outlet.

Exit velocity (feet/second) – The exit velocity of emissions through the exhaust outlet.

Exit temperature (degrees Fahrenheit) – The temperature of gaseous emissions measured at the exhaust outlet.

Outlet orientation (degrees) – The deviation of the exhaust outlet from vertically upward. 0 indicates an upward pointing outlet; 180 indicates a downward pointing outlet.

Emission controls – Indicates which common types of control devices are installed for this equipment.

A.4.3   Control Equipment Tab

Other control device? (yes/no) – Indicates whether additional controls are installed, other than the common control devices listed on the Exhaust System Tab.

Description – If present, a description of other control devices is required (other than those listed on the Exhaust System Tab).

SO_x efficiency (percent) – The total combined reductions in sulfur oxides emissions achieved by all other installed control devices (other than those listed on the Exhaust System Tab).

NO$_x$ efficiency (percent) – The total combined reductions in nitrogen oxides emissions achieved by all other installed control devices (other than those listed on the Exhaust System Tab).

CO efficiency (percent) – The total combined reductions in carbon monoxide emissions achieved by all other installed control devices (other than those listed on the Exhaust System Tab).

VOC efficiency (percent) – The total combined reductions in volatile organics emissions achieved by all other installed control devices (other than those listed on the Exhaust System Tab).

PM$_{10}$ efficiency (percent) – The total combined reductions in PM$_{10}$ emissions (particulate matter under 10 microns in diameter) achieved by all other installed control devices (other than those listed on the Exhaust System Tab).

A.4.4   QC Results Tab

Error Source – List of input variables for this equipment that have been flagged with QC error messages.

Error Description – List of the reasons that QC error messages were assigned.

Operator Comment – List of user's explanations for unusual or unexpected values that were flagged with QC error messages. An operator comment indicates that the user wishes to override the QC error message. (Select an error message, then click "Add QC Comment" in order to add Operator Comments.)

A.5   DIESEL OR GASOLINE ENGINE

A.5.1   General Information Tab

Engine elevation (feet above mean sea level) – The elevation of an engine, measured from mean sea level to its base.

Hours operated – The total number of hours that this engine was in operation during the specific monthly survey period.

Fuel type – The type of fuel burned by the equipment.

Fuel sulfur content (percent by mass) – The sulfur content in liquid fuel types.

Fuel heating value (British thermal units per pound) – The energy content of liquid fuel types.

Max rated horsepower (horsepower) – The manufacturer's maximum rated horsepower output.

Operating horsepower (horsepower) – The operating horsepower during operation this survey period.

Max rated fuel usage (British thermal units per horsepower-hour) – The manufacturer's maximum rate of fuel usage.

Average fuel usage (British thermal units per horsepower-hour) – The average rate of fuel usage during operation this survey period.

Total fuel used (gallons) – Total liquid fuel used during this survey period. If you do not monitor actual fuel use for an engine, a value may be calculated using:

[Hours operated * average fuel usage (Btu/hp-hr) * operating horsepower]÷[fuel heating value (19,300 Btu/lb) * (7.05 lbs/gal)].

Note that the fuel heating value and fuel density (7.05 lbs/gal) shown above are for diesel fuel.

No Emissions to Report - Indicates the status of the engine for the specific survey period.

- "No Emissions to Report" - Indicates that the equipment was unused for the entire month-long survey period.

Comments - A space for general user comments regarding this structure, with a maximum length of 255 characters.

A.5.2 Exhaust System Tab

Outlet height (feet above mean sea level) – The elevation of the stack outlet above mean sea level.

Outlet inner diameter (inches) – The inner diameter of the exhaust outlet.

Exit velocity (feet/second) – The exit velocity of emissions through the exhaust outlet.

Exit temperature (degrees Fahrenheit) – The temperature of gaseous emissions measured at the exhaust outlet.

Outlet orientation (degrees) – The deviation of the exhaust outlet from vertically upward. 0 indicates an upward pointing outlet; 180 indicates a downward pointing outlet.

A.5.3 Control Equipment Tab

Other control device? (yes/no) – Indicates whether additional controls are installed, other than the common control devices listed on the Exhaust System Tab.

Description – If present, a description of other control devices is required (other than those listed on the Exhaust System Tab).

SO_x efficiency (percent) – The total combined reductions in sulfur oxides emissions achieved by all other installed control devices (other than those listed on the Exhaust System Tab).

NO_x efficiency (percent) – The total combined reductions in nitrogen oxides emissions achieved by all other installed control devices (other than those listed on the Exhaust System Tab).

CO efficiency (percent) – The total combined reductions in carbon monoxide emissions achieved by all other installed control devices (other than those listed on the Exhaust System Tab).

VOC efficiency (percent) – The total combined reductions in volatile organics emissions achieved by all other installed control devices (other than those listed on the Exhaust System Tab).

PM_{10} efficiency (percent) – The total combined reductions in PM_{10} emissions (particulate matter under 10 microns in diameter) achieved by all other installed control devices (other than those listed on the Exhaust System Tab).

A.5.4   QC Results Tab

Error Source – List of input variables for this equipment that have been flagged with QC error messages.

Error Description – List of the reasons that QC error messages were assigned.

Operator Comment – List of user's explanations for unusual or unexpected values that were flagged with QC error messages. An operator comment indicates that the user wishes to override the QC error message. (Select an error message, then click "Add QC Comment" in order to add Operator Comments.)

A.6   DRILLING RIG

A.6.1   General Information Tab

Hours operated – The number of hours that a drilling rig was present and working at this structure.

Total diesel fuel usage (gallons) – The total diesel fuel used by the drilling rig during the survey period.

Total gasoline fuel usage (gallons) – The total gasoline fuel used by the drilling rig during the survey period.

Total natural gas fuel usage (thousand standard cubic feet) - The total natural gas used by the drilling rig during the survey period, volume adjusted to standard temperature and pressure (60 degrees Fahrenheit, 1 atmosphere).

No Emissions to Report – Indicates the status of the drilling rig for the specific survey period.

- "No Emissions to Report" - Indicates that the drilling rig was absent for the entire month-long survey period.

Comments - A space for general user comments regarding this structure, with a maximum length of 255 characters.

A.6.2   Control Equipment Tab

Other control device? (yes/no) – Indicates whether controls are installed.

Description – If present, a description of other control devices is required.

SO_x efficiency (percent) – The total combined reductions in sulfur oxides emissions achieved by all other installed control devices.

NO_x efficiency (percent) – The total combined reductions in nitrogen oxides emissions achieved by all other installed control devices.

CO efficiency (percent) – The total combined reductions in carbon monoxide emissions achieved by all other installed control devices.

VOC efficiency (percent) – The total combined reductions in volatile organics emissions achieved by all other installed control devices.

PM_{10} efficiency (percent) – The total combined reductions in PM_{10} emissions (particulate matter under 10 microns in diameter) achieved by all other installed control devices.

A.6.3   QC Results Tab

Error Source – List of input variables for this equipment that have been flagged with QC error messages.

Error Description – List of the reasons that QC error messages were assigned.

Operator Comment – List of user's explanations for unusual or unexpected values that were flagged with QC error messages. An operator comment indicates that the user wishes to override the QC error message. (Select an error message, then click "Add QC Comment" in order to add Operator Comments.)

A.7   COMBUSTION FLARE

A.7.1   General Information Tab

Note that flared emissions are combusted. If emissions are not combusted, create a Cold Vent record.

Hours operated, including upsets – The total number of hours that the flare was operated during the survey period, including periods of upset flaring.

Volume flared (thousand standard cubic feet), including upsets – The total volume of gas flared during the survey period, excluding periods of upset flaring, volume adjusted to standard temperature and pressure (60 degrees Fahrenheit, 1 atmosphere).

Flare gas H_2S Concentration (parts per million by volume) – The concentration of hydrogen sulfide present in the flare feed gas.

Is there a continuous pilot? (yes/no) – Indicates whether the flare stack is equipped with a continuos pilot light.

Pilot fuel feed rate (thousand standard cubic feet per day) – The feed rate of natural gas to a continuous pilot light.

Flare combustion efficiency (percent) – The flare combustion efficiency, or the completeness of hydrocarbon conversion to carbon dioxide (as CO_2).

Smoking condition – A qualitative assessment of the level of smoke emitted from the flare

- None (Soot emissions are approximately 0 pounds per million British thermal units of flare gas consumed.)

- Light (Soot emissions are approximately 40 pounds per million British thermal units of flare gas consumed.)

- Medium - (Soot emissions are approximately 177 pounds per million British thermal units of flare gas consumed.)

- Heavy - (Soot emissions are approximately 274 pounds per million British thermal units of flare gas consumed.)

Stack outlet elevation (feet above mean sea level) – The elevation of the flare stack outlet above mean sea level.

Stack inner diameter (inches) – The effective diameter of the flare stack at its outlet.

Average exit velocity (feet per second), excluding upsets – The average exit velocity of flare feed gas at the flare stack outlet during the survey period, excluding periods of upset conditions.

Average combustion temperature (degrees Fahrenheit) – The average flare combustion temperature during the survey period.

Stack orientation (degrees) - The deviation of the stack outlet from vertically upward. 0 indicates an upward pointing outlet; 180 indicates a downward pointing outlet.

No Emissions to Report – Indicates the status of the flare for the specific survey period.

- "No Emissions to Report" - Indicates that the flare was unused for the entire month-long survey period.

Comments - A space for general user comments regarding this structure, with a maximum length of 255 characters.

A.7.2   QC Results Tab

Error Source – List of input variables for this equipment that have been flagged with QC error messages.

Error Description – List of the reasons that QC error messages were assigned.

Operator Comment – List of user's explanations for unusual or unexpected values that were flagged with QC error messages. An operator comment indicates that the user wishes to override the QC error message. (Select an error message, then click "Add QC Comment" in order to add Operator Comments.)

A.8   FUGITIVES

A.8.1 General Information Tab

Stream type – Indicates the type of process stream handled by the set of components to be inventoried. (Components for different process streams at the same structure should be inventoried separately.)

- Light oil (API gravity ≥ 20°API)

- Heavy oil (API gravity<20°API)

- Oil/water mixture

- Oil/water/gas mixture

- Natural gas

- Natural gas liquids

Facility Size – Indicates a rough estimate of the total count of all components at this facility that handle the selected stream type.

Average VOC weight percent of fugitives – The average VOC content of fugitive emissions for the inventoried components and the selected stream type. You may find it beneficial to use the following information as a starting point.

Speciation Fractions for Total Hydrocarbon (THC) Emissions By Stream Type

THC Fraction	Gas	Light Oil (≥ 20 API Gravity)	Heavy Oil (<20 API Gravity)	Water/Oil*
Methane	0.945	0.612	0.942	0.612
Volatile Organic Compounds (VOC)	0.0137	0.296	0.030	0.296

* Water/oil refers to water streams in oil service with a water content greater than 50% from the point of origin to the point where the water content reaches 99%. For water streams with a water content greater than 99%, the emission rate is considered negligible.

Source: API, 1996. Calculation Workbook for Oil and Gas Production Equipment Fugitive Emissions.

Average equipment elevation (feet above mean sea level) – A good estimate is half the elevation of the top deck.

Equipment inventory (number of components) – An inventory of each type of component that handles the selected process stream at this structure. You are encouraged to prepare an equipment inventory by making direct counts of your components by service type.

Summary of Equipment Inventory Data (Number of Components) by Skid Type

Skid Type	Valves	Pump Seals	Threaded Connections	Flanges	Open Ended Lines	Compressor Seals*	Diaphragms	Drains	Dump Arms	Hatches	Instruments	Meters	Pressure Relief Valves	Polished Rods	Other Relief Valves
Separator Skid	34	0	13	73	0	0	0	2	0	0	15	1	1	0	0
Heater Treater Skid	98	0	70	114	0	0	0	3	0	0	25	0	3	0	0
LACT Charge Pump Skid	21	3	6	47	0	0	0	1	0	0	9	0	0	0	0
LACT Skid	62	1	75	69	0	0	0	1	0	0	34	4	6	0	0
Pipeline Pumps Skid	39	3	12	78	0	0	0	2	0	0	70	0	3	0	0
Pig Launcher/Receiver Skid	13	0	14	16	0	0	0	0	0	0	9	0	1	0	0
Compressor Skid	119	0	113	138	0	4	0	1	0	0	69	0	9	4	0
Filter/Separator Skid	30	0	25	37	0	0	0	1	0	0	9	0	1	0	0
Gas Dehydration Skid	23	0	14	40	0	0	0	1	0	0	12	0	1	0	0
Glycol Regeneration Skid	134	0	110	194	0	0	0	4	0	0	45	1	7	6	1
Gas Meter	10	0	11	26	0	0	0	1	0	0	21	2	0	0	0
Fuel Gas Skid	62	0	47	85	0	0	0	1	0	0	32	1	4	0	0
Flotation Cell Skid	41	1	34	70	0	0	1	1	0	15	8	0	2	0	2
Scrubber	13	0	13	18	0	0	0	1	0	0	9	0	1	0	0
Amine Unit	226	8	166	391	0	0	1	5	0	0	121	2	12	0	1
Line Heater	30	0	46	18	0	0	0	1	0	0	10	0	0	0	1
Production Manifold	108	0	31	148	0	0	0	1	0	0	43	0	0	7	0
Wellhead	15	0	6	19	0	0	0	0	0	0	11	0	0	0	0
Import or Export Pipeline	3	0	0	9	0	0	0	0	0	0	0	0	0	0	0

* Because there is a large variation in emissions for compressor seals, you are asked to specify the compressor and seal type:
- Centrifugal- wet seal;
- Centrifugal- dry seal;
- Reciprocating- shaft packing; or Other (specify).

You may find it beneficial to use of the following information as a starting point, however. This information was compiled for MMS by the Offshore Operators Committee, and can be adjusted by service type for each component for each part of the production train (i.e., for each skid type). Counts must be reported for each service type (gas, heavy oil, light oil, oil/water).

Comments – A space for general user comments regarding this structure, with a maximum length of 255 characters.

A.8.2   QC Results Tab

Error Source – List of input variables for this equipment that have been flagged with QC error messages.

Error Description – List of the reasons that QC error messages were assigned.

Operator Comment – List of user's explanations for unusual or unexpected values that were flagged with QC error messages. An operator comment indicates that the user wishes to override the QC error message. (Select an error message, then click "Add QC Comment" in order to add Operator Comments.)

A.9 GLYCOL DEHYDRATOR UNIT

A.9.1 General Information Tab

Note that the fire tube is considered to be a boiler/heater/burner. Information about the fire tube should be entered on the data entry screen for boiler/heater/burner. Access the boiler/heater/burner data entry screen by selecting Edit|New Equipment from the GOADS main menu. Select "Boiler, Heater, or Burner" as the new equipment type.

Also note that recovered vapors, which are combusted elsewhere at the facility, should be accounted for by the equipment type where they are combusted. Vapors that are vented or flared locally or that are collected into the facility manifold system may be accounted for on the Ventilation System Tab.

Processed throughput (million standard cubic feet) – The total volume of natural gas processed by this glycol unit during the specific monthly survey period, volume adjusted to standard temperature and pressure (60 degrees Fahrenheit, 1 atmosphere).

Hours operated – The total number of hours that this glycol unit was in operation during the specific monthly survey period.

Glycol unit elevation (feet above mean sea level) – The elevation of the glycol unit, measured from mean sea level to its base.

Glycol type (TEG/EG) – Indicates the type of glycol used in this unit, triethylene glycol (TEG) or ethylene glycol (EG).

Glycol circulation rate (gallons per minute) – The actual rate of glycol circulation through the glycol unit.

Glycol pump type (electric/gas) – The type of pump that drives glycol circulation.

Lean glycol H_2O content (percent by weight) – The water content of the lean, or recharged, glycol.

Is the unprocessed gas saturated (yes/no) – Indicates if the unprocessed gas is saturated with water.

Wet gas H_2O content (pounds per million standard cubic feet) – The water content of the natural gas prior to glycol dehydration.

Dry gas H_2O content (pounds per million standard cubic feet) – The water content of the natural gas following glycol dehydration.

Wet gas temperature (degrees Fahrenheit) – The temperature of the natural gas prior to glycol dehydration.

Wet gas pressure (pounds per square inch gauge) – The pressure of the natural gas prior to glycol dehydration.

Cold separator temperature (degrees Fahrenheit) – The temperature of the combined gas and glycol downstream of any refrigeration. If no refrigeration is present, then this is the temperature downstream from the separator.

Cold separator pressure (pounds per square inch gauge) – The pressure of the combined gas and glycol downstream of any refrigeration. If no refrigeration is present, then this is the pressure downstream from the separator.

Unprocessed natural gas concentrations (percent by volume) – The volumetric concentrations of constituents present in the unprocessed natural gas stream, including the following:

- Hydrogen Sulfide
- Methane (CH_4)
- Ethane (C_2H_6)
- C3 Hydrocarbons (hydrocarbons with 3 carbon atoms in their molecular structure)
- C4 Hydrocarbons
- C5 Hydrocarbons
- C6 Hydrocarbons
- C7 Hydrocarbons
- C8+ Hydrocarbons (hydrocarbons with 8 or more carbon atoms in their molecular structure)

In addition, please report concentrations (percent by volume) for the following constituents if the data are readily available. It is not mandatory that you enter this data:

- Benzene
- Toluene
- Ethylbenzene
- Xylenes
- n-Hexane
- 2,2,4-Trimethylpentane

Equipped with a flash tank? (yes/no) – Indicates whether the system is equipped with a flash tank (or separator) that vents to the atmosphere.

Destination of flash gas – Indicates if the gas is routed back into the system, vented to the atmosphere, or burned in a flare.

Flash tank temperature (degrees Fahrenheit) – The temperature of the flash tank.

Flash tank pressure (pounds per square inch gauge) – The pressure of the flash tank.

Uses stripping gas? – Indicates what type of stripping gas (if any) is used in the regenerator to improve water removal from the rich glycol.

- None
- Dry gas
- Flash gas – Exhaust from the flash tank
- Nitrogen – From a nitrogen supply

Stripping gas flow rate (standard cubic feet per minute) – The flow rate of stripping gas to the regenerator, volume adjusted to standard temperature and pressure (60 degrees Fahrenheit, 1 atmosphere).

No Emissions to Report – Indicates the status of the glycol dehydrator for the specific survey period.

- "No Emissions to Report" - Indicates that the equipment was unused for the entire month-long survey period.

Comments - A space for general user comments regarding this structure, with a maximum length of 255 characters.

A.9.2   Ventilation System Tab – For Still Column Vent Only

Emissions destination – Indicates whether the emissions from this equipment are vented or flared locally, or at some distance from the equipment.

Low-pressure vent/flare ID – Indicates the destination vent or flare identifier code (if emissions are not vented or flared locally). It may be necessary to first create a vent or flare before it will appear in the list (using the Edit|New Equipment menu).

Outlet height (feet above mean sea level) – The elevation of the stack outlet above mean sea level.

Outlet inner diameter (inches) – The inner diameter of a process vent/flare.

Exit velocity (feet/second) – The exit velocity of emissions through the outlet of a process vent/flare.

Exit temperature (degrees Fahrenheit) – The temperature of gaseous emissions measured at the outlet of a process vent.

Outlet orientation (degrees) – The deviation of the outlet from vertically upward. 0 indicates an upward pointing outlet; 180 indicates a downward pointing outlet.

Flare feed rate (standard cubic feet per hour) – The volumetric feed rate to a process flare.

Combustion temperature (degrees Fahrenheit) – The combustion temperature of a process flare.

Combustion efficiency (percent) – The combustion efficiency of a process flare, or the completeness of hydrocarbon conversion to carbon dioxide (as CO_2).

Installed control equipment – Indicates which common types of control devices are installed for this equipment.

Condenser temperature (degrees Fahrenheit) – The operating temperature of a condenser installed as a control device.

Condenser pressure (absolute pounds per square inch) – The operating temperature of a condenser installed as a control device.

A.9.3   Control Equipment Tab

Other control device? (yes/no) – Indicates whether additional controls are installed, other than the common control devices listed on the Ventilation System Tab.

Description – If present, a description of other control devices is required (other than those listed on the Ventilation System Tab).

SO_x efficiency (percent) – The total combined reductions in sulfur oxides emissions achieved by all other installed control devices (other than those listed on the Ventilation System Tab).

NO_x efficiency (percent) – The total combined reductions in nitrogen oxides emissions achieved by all other installed control devices (other than those listed on the Ventilation System Tab).

CO efficiency (percent) – The total combined reductions in carbon monoxide emissions achieved by all other installed control devices (other than those listed on the Ventilation System Tab).

VOC efficiency (percent) – The total combined reductions in volatile organics emissions achieved by all other installed control devices (other than those listed on the Ventilation System Tab).

PM_{10} efficiency (percent) – The total combined reductions in PM_{10} emissions (particulate matter under 10 microns in diameter) achieved by all other installed control devices (other than those listed on the Ventilation System Tab).

A.9.4   QC Results Tab

Error Source – List of input variables for this equipment that have been flagged with QC error messages.

Error Description – List of the reasons that QC error messages were assigned.

Operator Comment – List of user's explanations for unusual or unexpected values that were flagged with QC error messages. An operator comment indicates that the user wishes to override the QC error message. (Select an error message, then click "Add QC Comment" in order to add Operator Comments.)

A.10   LOADING OPERATION

A.10.1   General Information Tab

Volume loaded (barrels) – The quantity of liquid hydrocarbon loaded into ships or barges at this structure.

Average elevation (feet above mean sea level) – The approximate elevation of loading operations, measured from mean sea level to the point of the receiving vessel.

Storage tank paint color – The exterior paint color of the receiving storage tank.

Storage tank paint condition – The exterior paint condition of the receiving storage tank.

Bulk liquid temperature (degrees Fahrenheit) – The bulk temperature of the liquid contained within the receiving storage tank.

Product Reid vapor pressure (absolute pounds per square inch) – The Reid vapor pressure of the liquid contained within the receiving storage tank.

Average percent by weight of VOCs in tank vapor (percent) – The VOC content of vapors in the storage tank headspace, measured as weight percent.

Average molecular weight of VOCs in tank vapor (pounds per pound-mol) – The average molecular weight of VOCs present in the storage tank headspace.

No Emissions to Report – Indicates the status of the loading operations for the specific survey period.

- "No Emissions to Report" - Indicates that no loading operations occurred for the entire month-long survey period.

Comments - A space for general user comments regarding this structure, with a maximum length of 255 characters.

A.10.2   Ventilation System Tab

Emissions destination – Indicates whether the emissions from this equipment are vented or flared locally, or at some distance from the equipment.

Low-pressure vent/flare ID – Indicates the destination vent or flare identifier code (if emissions are not vented or flared locally). It may be necessary to first create a vent or flare before it will appear in the list (using the Edit|New Equipment menu).

Outlet height (feet above mean sea level) – The elevation of the stack outlet above mean sea level.

Outlet inner diameter (inches) – The inner diameter of a process vent/flare.

Exit velocity (feet/second) – The exit velocity of emissions through the outlet of a process vent/flare.

Exit temperature (degrees Fahrenheit) – The temperature of gaseous emissions measured at the outlet of a process vent.

Outlet orientation (degrees) – The deviation of the outlet from vertically upward. 0 indicates an upward pointing outlet; 180 indicates a downward pointing outlet.

Flare feed rate (standard cubic feet per hour) – The volumetric feed rate to a process flare.

Combustion temperature (degrees Fahrenheit) – The combustion temperature of a process flare.

Combustion efficiency (percent) – The combustion efficiency of a process flare, or the completeness of hydrocarbon conversion to carbon dioxide (as CO_2).

Installed control equipment – Indicates which common types of control devices are installed for this equipment.

A.10.3 Control Equipment Tab

Other control device? (yes/no) – Indicates whether additional controls are installed, other than the common control devices listed on the Ventilation System Tab.

Description – If present, a description of other control devices is required (other than those listed on the Ventilation System Tab).

VOC efficiency (percent) – The total combined reductions in volatile organics emissions achieved by all other installed control devices (other than those listed on the Ventilation System Tab).

A.10.4 QC Results Tab

Error Source – List of input variables for this equipment that have been flagged with QC error messages.

Error Description – List of the reasons that QC error messages were assigned.

Operator Comment – List of user's explanations for unusual or unexpected values that were flagged with QC error messages. An operator comment indicates that the user wishes to override the QC error message. (Select an error message, then click "Add QC Comment" in order to add Operator Comments.)

A.11   LOSSES FROM FLASHING

A.11.1   General Information Tab

Type of vessel – Indicates the type of vessel (separator, heater treater, surge tank, storage tank, other) where the flashing occurs.

API gravity of stored oil (degrees API) – The API gravity of the oil/condensate contained within the vessel where the flashing occurs.

Operating pressure of vessel (pounds per square inch gauge)– Indicates the pressure setting of the vessel where the flashing occurs.

Operating temperature of vessel (degrees Fahrenheit) – Indicates the operating temperature of the vessel where the flashing occurs.

Oil/condensate throughput (barrels) – Indicates the actual throughput volume of oil/condensate for each vessel for the specific monthly survey period.

Operating pressure immediately upstream of vessel (pounds per square inch gauge) – Indicates the operating pressure upstream of the vessel.

Operating temperature immediately upstream of vessel (degrees Fahrenheit) – Indicates the operating temperature upstream of the vessel.

Standard cubic feet of flash per barrel of oil (SCF/barrel) – If data are readily available, indicate the SCF of flash per barrel of oil/condensate specific to your source. It is not mandatory that you that you enter this data.

No Emissions to Report – Indicates the status of the vessel for the specific survey period.

- "No Emissions to Report" - Indicates that the vessel was empty and unused for the entire month-long survey period.

Comments – A space for general user comments regarding this structure, with a maximum length of 255 characters.

A.11.2   Ventilation System Tab

Emissions destination – Indicates whether the emissions from this equipment are vented or flared locally, or at some distance from the equipment.

Low-pressure vent/flare ID – Indicates the destination vent or flare identifier code (if emissions are not vented or flared locally). It may be necessary to first create a vent or flare before it will appear in the list (using the Edit|New Equipment menu).

Outlet height (feet above mean sea level) – The elevation of the stack outlet above mean sea level.

Outlet inner diameter (inches) – The inner diameter of a process vent.

Exit velocity (feet/second) – The exit velocity of emissions through the outlet of a process vent.

Exit temperature (degrees Fahrenheit) – The temperature of gaseous emissions measured at the outlet of a process vent.

Outlet orientation (degrees) – The deviation of the outlet from vertically upward. 0 indicates an upward pointing outlet; 180 indicates a downward pointing outlet.

A.11.3 QC Results Tab

Error Source – List of input variables for this equipment that have been flagged with QC error messages.

Error Description – List of the reasons that QC error messages were assigned.

Operator Comment – List of user's explanations for unusual or unexpected values that were flagged with QC error messages. An operator comment indicates that the user wishes to override the QC error message. (Select an error message, then click "Add QC Comment" in order to add Operator Comments.)

A.12 MUD DEGASSING

A.12.1 General Information Tab

Days per month of drilling with mud (i.e., drilling fluid) – The total number of 24-hour days that drilling (with mud) occurred during the specific monthly survey period.

Type of mud – Indicates the type of mud used (drilling fluid) (water-based, oil-based, or synthetic).

No Emissions to Report – Indicates the status of the operation for the specific survey period.

- "No Emissions to Report" – Indicates that the equipment was unused for the entire month-long survey period.

Comments – A space for general user comments regarding this structure, with a maximum length of 255 characters.

A.12.2 QC Results Tab

Error Source – List of input variables for this equipment that have been flagged with QC error messages.

Error Description – List of the reasons that QC error messages were assigned.

Operator Comment – List of user's explanations for unusual or unexpected values that were flagged with QC error messages. An operator comment indicates that the user wishes to override the QC error message. (Select an error message, then click "Add QC Comment" in order to add Operator Comments.)

A.13 NATURAL GAS ENGINE

A.13.1 General Information Tab

Engine elevation (feet above mean sea level) – The elevation of an engine, measured from mean sea level to its base.

Hours operated – The total number of hours that this engine was in operation during the specific monthly survey period.

Manufacturer – The company name of the engine manufacturer.

Model No. – The manufacturer's model number of the engine.

Engine stroke – Indicates whether the engine is a 2-stroke design or a 4-stroke design.

Engine burn – Indicates the fuel burn conditions (lean-burn, rich-burn, or clean-burn).

Fuel H_2S content (parts per million by volume) – The concentration of hydrogen sulfide in gaseous fuel types.

Fuel heating value (British thermal units per standard cubic feet) – The energy content of gaseous fuel types.

Max rated horsepower (horsepower) – The manufacturer's maximum rated horsepower output.

Operating horsepower (horsepower) – The operating horsepower during operation this survey period.

Max rated fuel usage (British thermal units per horsepower-hour) – The manufacturer's maximum rate of fuel usage.

Average fuel usage (British thermal units per horsepower-hour) – The average rate of fuel usage during operation this survey period.

Total fuel used (thousand standard cubic feet) – Total gaseous fuel used during this survey period, volume adjusted to standard temperature and pressure (60 degrees Fahrenheit, 1 atmosphere). If you do not monitor actual fuel use for an engine, a value may be calculated using:

[Hours operated * average fuel usage (Btu/hp-hr) * operating horsepower]÷[fuel heating value (1,050 Btu/scf) * (1,000 scf/Mscf)].

No Emissions to Report – Indicates the status of the engine for the specific survey period.

- "No Emissions to Report" – Indicates that the equipment was unused for the entire month-long survey period.

Comments – A space for general user comments regarding this structure, with a maximum length of 255 characters.

A.13.2 Exhaust System Tab

Outlet height (feet above mean sea level) – The elevation of the stack outlet above mean sea level.

Outlet inner diameter (inches) – The inner diameter of the exhaust outlet.

Exit velocity (feet/second) – The exit velocity of emissions through the exhaust outlet.

Exit temperature (degrees Fahrenheit) – The temperature of gaseous emissions measured at the exhaust outlet.

Outlet orientation (degrees) – The deviation of the exhaust outlet from vertically upward. 0 indicates an upward pointing outlet; 180 indicates a downward pointing outlet.

A.13.3 Control Equipment Tab

Other control device? (yes/no) – Indicates whether additional controls are installed.

Description – If present, a description of other control devices is required.

SO_x efficiency (percent) – The total combined reductions in sulfur oxides emissions achieved by all other installed control devices.

NO_x efficiency (percent) – The total combined reductions in nitrogen oxides emissions achieved by all other installed control devices.

CO efficiency (percent) – The total combined reductions in carbon monoxide emissions achieved by all other installed control devices.

VOC efficiency (percent) – The total combined reductions in volatile organic compound emissions achieved by all other installed control devices.

PM_{10} efficiency (percent) – The total combined reductions in PM_{10} emissions (particulate matter under 10 microns in diameter) achieved by all other installed control devices.

A.13.4 QC Results Tab

Error Source – List of input variables for this equipment that have been flagged with QC error messages.

Error Description – List of the reasons that QC error messages were assigned.

Operator Comment – List of user's explanations for unusual or unexpected values that were flagged with QC error messages. An operator comment indicates that the user wishes to override the QC error message. (Select an error message, then click "Add QC Comment" in order to add Operator Comments.)

A.14 NATURAL GAS TURBINE

A.14.1 General Information Tab

Engine elevation (feet above mean sea level) – The elevation of a natural gas turbine, measured from mean sea level to its base.

Hours operated – The total number of hours that this turbine was in operation during the specific monthly survey period.

Manufacturer – The company name of the turbine manufacturer.

Model No. – The manufacturer's model number of the turbine.

Engine purpose of use – The purpose for which this turbine is used.

- Electricity Generation
- Product Pressurization
- Other

Fuel H_2S content (parts per million by volume) – The concentration of hydrogen sulfide in gaseous fuel types.

Fuel heating value (British thermal units per standard cubic feet) – The energy content of gaseous fuel types.

Max rated horsepower (horsepower) – The manufacturer's maximum rated horsepower output.

Operating horsepower (horsepower) – The operating horsepower during operation this survey period.

Max rated fuel usage (British thermal units per horsepower-hour) – The manufacturer's maximum rate of fuel usage.

Average fuel usage (British thermal units per horsepower-hour) – The average rate of fuel usage during operation this survey period.

Total fuel used (thousand standard cubic feet) – Total gaseous fuel used during this survey period, volume adjusted to standard temperature and pressure (60 degrees Fahrenheit, 1 atmosphere). If you do not monitor actual fuel use for a turbine, a value may be calculated using:

[Hours operated * average fuel usage (Btu/hp-hr) * operating horsepower]÷[fuel heating value (1,050 Btu/scf) * (1,000 scf/Mscf)].

No Emissions to Report – Indicates the status of the turbine for the specific survey period.

- "No Emissions to Report" – Indicates that the equipment was unused for the entire month-long survey period.

Comments – A space for general user comments regarding this structure, with a maximum length of 255 characters.

A.14.2 Exhaust System Tab

Outlet height (feet above mean sea level) – The elevation of the stack outlet above mean sea level.

Outlet inner diameter (inches) – The inner diameter of the exhaust outlet.

Exit velocity (feet/second) – The exit velocity of emissions through the exhaust outlet.

Exit temperature (degrees Fahrenheit) – The temperature of gaseous emissions measured at the exhaust outlet.

Outlet orientation (degrees) – The deviation of the exhaust outlet from vertically upward. 0 indicates an upward pointing outlet; 180 indicates a downward pointing outlet.

A.14.3 Control Equipment Tab

Other control device? (yes/no) – Indicates whether additional controls are installed, other than the common control devices listed on the Exhaust System Tab.

Description – If present, a description of other control devices is required (other than those listed on the Exhaust System Tab).

SO_x efficiency (percent) – The total combined reductions in sulfur oxides emissions achieved by all other installed control devices (other than those listed on the Exhaust System Tab).

NO_x efficiency (percent) – The total combined reductions in nitrogen oxides emissions achieved by all other installed control devices (other than those listed on the Exhaust System Tab).

CO efficiency (percent) – The total combined reductions in carbon monoxide emissions achieved by all other installed control devices (other than those listed on the Exhaust System Tab).

VOC efficiency (percent) – The total combined reductions in volatile organics emissions achieved by all other installed control devices (other than those listed on the Exhaust System Tab).

PM_{10} efficiency (percent) – The total combined reductions in PM_{10} emissions (particulate matter under 10 microns in diameter) achieved by all other installed control devices (other than those listed on the Exhaust System Tab).

A.14.4 QC Results Tab

Error Source – List of input variables for this equipment that have been flagged with QC error messages.

Error Description – List of the reasons that QC error messages were assigned.

Operator Comment – List of user's explanations for unusual or unexpected values that were flagged with QC error messages. An operator comment indicates that the user wishes to override the QC error message. (Select an error message, then click "Add QC Comment" in order to add Operator Comments.)

A.15   PNEUMATIC PUMPS

A.15.1   General Information Tab

Manufacturer – The company name of the equipment manufacturer. Examples include: Wilden diaphragm pumps (M-1, M-2, M-4, M-8, M-15); and Texsteam chemical injection and diaphragm pumps.

Model – The manufacturer's model number of the pump. Only include pumps that are in natural gas service. Do not include pumps in compressed air service.

Fuel usage rate (standard cubic feet per hour) – The rate of natural gas usage during operation this survey period. If this information is not readily available, it is not mandatory that you enter this data.

Hours operated – The total number of hours that the pump was in operation during the specific monthly survey period.

Pump elevation (feet above mean sea level) – The approximate elevation of the pump, measured from mean sea level to its base.

No Emissions to Report – Indicates the status of the pump for the specific survey period.

- "No Emissions to Report" – Indicates that the pump was unused for the entire month-long survey period.

Comments – A space for general user comments regarding this structure, with a maximum length of 255 characters.

A.15.2   Ventilation System Tab

Emissions destination – Indicates whether the emissions from this equipment are vented or flared locally, or at some distance from the equipment.

Low-pressure vent/flare ID – Indicates the destination vent or flare identifier code (if emissions are not vented or flared locally). It may be necessary to first create

Outlet height (feet above mean sea level) – The elevation of the stack outlet above mean sea level.

Outlet inner diameter (inches) – The inner diameter of a process vent.

Exit velocity (feet/second) – The exit velocity of emissions through the outlet of a process vent.

Exit temperature (degrees Fahrenheit) – The temperature of gaseous emissions measured at the outlet of a process vent.

Outlet orientation (degrees) – The deviation of the outlet from vertically upward. 0 indicates an upward pointing outlet; 180 indicates a downward pointing outlet.

A.15.3 QC Results Tab

Error Source – List of input variables for this equipment that have been flagged with QC error messages.

Error Description – List of the reasons that QC error messages were assigned.

Operator Comment – List of user's explanations for unusual or unexpected values that were flagged with QC error messages. An operator comment indicates that the user wishes to override the QC error message. (Select an error message, then click "Add QC Comment" in order to add Operator Comments.)

A.16. PRESSURE/LEVEL CONTROLLERS

A.16.1 General Information Tab

Service Type – Indicates whether the equipment is in pressure control or level control service.

Manufacturer – The company name of the equipment manufacturer. Only include equipment that is in natural gas service. Do not include equipment in compressed air service.

Model – The manufacturer's model number of the equipment.

Number of this make-model – Number of equipment of this exact make and model.

Fuel usage rate (standard cubic feet per hour) – The rate of natural gas usage during operation this survey period. If this information is not readily available, it is not mandatory that you enter this data.

Hours operated – The total number of hours that the equipment was in operation during the specific monthly survey period.

Equipment elevation (feet above mean sea level) – A good estimate is half the elevation of the top deck.

No Emissions to Report – Indicates the status of the equipment operations for the specific survey period.

- "No Emissions to Report" - Indicates that the equipment was unused for the entire month-long survey period.

Comments – A space for general user comments regarding this structure, with a maximum length of 255 characters.

A.16.2 QC Results Tab

Error Source – List of input variables for this equipment that have been flagged with QC error messages.

Error Description – List of the reasons that QC error messages were assigned.

A.17. STORAGE TANK

A.17.1 General Information Tab

Product throughput (barrels) – The volume of liquid hydrocarbon turned over through the storage tank during the survey period.

Tank elevation (feet above mean sea level) – The elevation of a storage tank, measured from mean sea level to its base.

Tank orientation (horizontal/vertical) – Indicates whether the tank is elongated and narrow in the horizontal direction (horizontal), or otherwise (vertical).

Tank shape (cylindrical/rectangular) – Indicates whether the tank is cylindrical or rectangular in shape.

Average liquid height (feet) – The average height of stored liquid during the survey period, measured from the bottom of the storage space to the top of the liquid.

Tank shell diameter (feet) – The diameter of a cylindrical tank (either horizontal or vertical).

Tank shell height (feet) – The vertical height of a cylindrical tank (oriented vertically) or of a rectangular tank (oriented vertically or horizontally).

Tank shell length (feet) – The longest horizontal dimension of a horizontal tank.

Tank shell width (feet) – The horizontal width of a rectangular tank (oriented vertically or horizontally).

2nd Tank shell width (feet) – The 2nd horizontal width of a rectangular tank (oriented vertically).

Is the roof fixed (not floating)? (yes/no) – Indicates whether the tank has a fixed or floating roof.

Roof shape – Indicates the shape of a vertical tank's roof.

- Cone – cylindrical tanks
- Dome – cylindrical tanks
- Flat – cylindrical or rectangular
- Peaked – rectangular

Roof height above shell (feet) – The height of a fixed roof measured from the top of the tank shell to the highest point of the roof.

Breather vent pressure setting (pounds per square inch gauge) – The pressure setting of the tank breather valve.

Breather vent vacuum setting (pounds per square inch gauge) – The vacuum setting of the tank breather valve.

Paint color – The exterior paint color of the storage tank.

Paint condition – The exterior paint condition of the storage tank.

Bulk liquid temperature (degrees Fahrenheit) – The bulk temperature of the liquid contained within the storage tank.

Product type (crude/condensate) – Indicates whether the storage tank contains crude oil or condensates. It is not mandatory that you enter data for jet fuel storage tanks.

API gravity (degrees API) – The API gravity of the liquid contained within the storage tank.

Product Reid vapor pressure (absolute pounds per square inch) – The Reid vapor pressure of the liquid contained within the storage tank.

Average percent by weight of VOCs in tank vapor (percent) – The VOC content of vapors in the storage tank headspace, measured as weight percent.

Average molecular weight of VOCs in tank vapor (pounds per pound-mol) – The average molecular weight of VOCs present in the storage tank headspace.

Equipped with a flash tank? (yes/no) – Indicates whether the storage tank is equipped with an upstream flash tank.

No Emissions to Report – Indicates the status of the storage for the specific survey period.

- "No Emissions to Report" – Indicates that the tank was empty and unused for the entire month-long survey period.

Comments – A space for general user comments regarding this structure, with a maximum length of 255 characters.

A.17.2 Ventilation System Tab

Emissions destination – Indicates whether the emissions from this equipment are vented or flared locally, or at some distance from the equipment.

Low-pressure vent/flare ID – Indicates the destination vent or flare identifier code (if emissions are not vented or flared locally). It may be necessary to first create

Outlet height (feet above mean sea level) – The elevation of the stack outlet above mean sea level.

Outlet inner diameter (inches) – The inner diameter of a process vent or the effective diameter of a flare.

Exit velocity (feet/second) – The exit velocity of emissions through the outlet of a process vent/flare.

Exit temperature (degrees Fahrenheit) – The temperature of gaseous emissions measured at the outlet of a process vent.

Outlet orientation (degrees) – The deviation of the outlet from vertically upward. 0 indicates an upward pointing outlet; 180 indicates a downward pointing outlet.

Flare feed rate (standard cubic feet per hour) – The volumetric feed rate to a process flare.

Combustion temperature (degrees Fahrenheit) – The combustion temperature of a process flare.

Combustion efficiency (percent) – The combustion efficiency of a process flare, or the completeness of hydrocarbon conversion to carbon dioxide (as CO_2).

Installed control equipment – Indicates which common types of control devices are installed for this equipment.

Condenser temperature (degrees Fahrenheit) – The operating temperature of a condenser installed as a control device.

Condenser pressure (absolute pounds per square inch) – The operating pressure of a condenser installed as a control device.

A.17.3 Control Equipment Tab

Other control device? (yes/no) – Indicates whether additional controls are installed, other than the common control devices listed on the Ventilation System Tab.

Description – If present, a description of other control devices is required (other than those listed on the Ventilation System Tab).

VOC efficiency (percent) – The total combined reductions in volatile organics emissions achieved by all other installed control devices (other than those listed on the Ventilation System Tab).

A.17.4 QC Results Tab

Error Source – List of input variables for this equipment that have been flagged with QC error messages.

Error Description – List of the reasons that QC error messages were assigned.

Operator Comment – List of user's explanations for unusual or unexpected values that were flagged with QC error messages. An operator comment indicates that the user wishes to override the QC error message. (Select an error message, then click "Add QC Comment" in order to add Operator Comments.)

A.18 COLD VENT

A.18.1 General Information Tab

Note that vented emissions are NOT combusted. If emissions are combusted, create a Combustion Flare record.

Hours operated, including upsets – The total number of hours that the vent was operated during the survey period, including periods of upset venting.

Volume vented (thousand standard cubic feet), including upsets – The total volume of gas vented during the survey period, including periods of upset venting, volume adjusted to standard temperature and pressure (60 degrees Fahrenheit, 1 atmosphere).

Vent type – Indicates whether vent gases are released at high pressure or low pressure.

Vent gas H_2S Concentration (parts per million by volume) – The concentration of hydrogen sulfide present in the vented gas.

Vent gas VOC Concentration (parts per million by volume) – The concentration of volatile organic compounds present in the vented gas.

Average molecular weight of VOCs (lb/lb-mol) – The average molecular weight of VOCs present in the vented gas.

Stack outlet elevation (feet above mean sea level) – The elevation of the vent stack outlet above mean sea level.

Stack inner diameter (inches) – The inner diameter of the vent stack at its outlet.

Average exit velocity (feet per second) – The average exit velocity of vented gas at the stack outlet.

Exit temperature (degrees Fahrenheit) – The average temperature of vented gas at the stack outlet.

Stack orientation (degrees) – The deviation of the stack outlet from vertically upward. 0 indicates an upward pointing outlet; 180 indicates a downward pointing outlet.

Installed control equipment – Indicates which common types of control devices are installed on the vent.

Condenser temperature (degrees Fahrenheit) – The operating temperature of a condenser installed as a control device.

Condenser pressure (absolute pounds per square inch) – The operating pressure of a condenser installed as a control device.

No Emissions to Report – Indicates the status of the vent for the specific survey period.

- "No Emissions to Report" – Indicates that the vent was unused for the entire month-long survey period.

Comments – A space for general user comments regarding this structure, with a maximum length of 255 characters.

A.18.2 Control Equipment Tab

Other control device? (yes/no) – Indicates whether controls are installed.

Description – If present, a description of other control devices is required.

VOC efficiency (percent) – The total combined reductions in volatile organics emissions achieved by all other installed control devices.

A.18.3 QC Results Tab

Error Source – List of input variables for this equipment that have been flagged with QC error messages.

Error Description – List of the reasons that QC error messages were assigned.

Operator Comment – List of user's explanations for unusual or unexpected values that were flagged with QC error messages. An operator comment indicates that the user wishes to override the QC error message. (Select an error message, then click "Add QC Comment" in order to add Operator Comments.)

APPENDIX B

GOADS-2005 QA SUMMARY FORM DATA FIELDS

This appendix indicates the data fields that will be flagged in the QA Summary Form if they are missing or inconsistent from month to month. If all of your GOADS-2005 entries are complete and the values are within two standard deviations of the average for all values in that field, the QA Summary Form will be blank.

The data fields in the QA Summary Form are critical to developing emission estimates. If an element appears on the QA Summary Form printout, you should re-evaluate your GOADS-2005 file and complete or correct the data you entered for the equipment or month shown. If the flagged value is legitimate, you may annotate the QA Summary Form using colored ink, or attach additional sheets which specify why a value is valid and does not need to be changed.

You must print out the GOADS-2005 QA Summary Form and submit it with your data files. If any values are flagged as incomplete or inconsistent, MMS will contact you. Please make sure you review the QA Summary Form closely, correct and errors that are flagged, and use the comment field for flagged entries that are valid. The following table lists the type codes used on the QA Summary Form.

GOADS-2005 QA Summary Form
Equipment Type Codes

AMI   =   Amine gas sweetening unit

BOI   =   Boiler/heater/burner

DIE   =   Diesel or gasoline engine

DRI   =   Drilling rig

FLA   =   Combustion Flare

FUG   =   Fugitives

GLY   =   Glycol dehydrator unit

LOA   =   Loading operation

LOS   =   Losses from flashing

MUD   =   Mud degassing

NGE   =   Natural gas engine

NGT   =   Natural gas turbine

PNE   =   Pneumatic pumps

PRE   =   Pressure/level controllers

STO   =   Storage tank

VEN   =   Cold Vent

GOADS-2005 QA Summary Form Data Fields

SURVEY LEVEL	Operator Comments
General Operator Information	
User name and phone number	
Company name	
Survey Information	
Operator identified	
12 surveys included	
Structure Information	
Area/Block/Name	
Longitude/latitude	
Distance to shore	
Gas production	
Crude oil production	
Natural gas usage for all 12 months consistent with survey data	
Diesel fuel usage for all 12 months consistent with survey data	
Gasoline usage for all 12 months consistent with survey data	
Number and unique pieces of equipment consistent for all 12 mos.	
Sales gas composition	

GOADS-2005 QA Summary Form Data Fields (Continued)

SURVEY LEVEL	Operator Comments
Equipment Information	
Amine Gas Sweetening Unit	
Processed throughput	
Hours operated	
Unprocessed natural gas concentration (% by volume)	
Quantity emitted when uncontrolled (%)	
Amine type*	
Equipped with a flash tank (yes/no)*	
Disposition of flash gas*	
Vented into low-pressure system	
Gases vented or flared	
Boilers/heaters/burners	
Fuel type	
Maximum rated heat input	
Hours of operated	
Average heat input	
Control device identified	
Same equipment units reported for each month/survey	

B-6

GOADS-2005 QA Summary Form Data Fields (Continued)

SURVEY LEVEL	Operator Comments
Diesel or Gasoline Engines	
Fuel type	
Maximum rated horsepower	
Hours operated	
Operating horsepower	
Maximum rated fuel usage	
Average fuel usage	
Control device identified	
Same equipment units reported for each month/survey	
Drilling Rig	
Hours operated	
Total diesel fuel usage	
Total gasoline usage	
Total natural gas fuel usage	
Combustion Flare	
Volume flared reported for continuous and episodic flaring	
Continuous pilot	
Pilot fuel feed rate	

GOADS-2005 QA Summary Form Data Fields (Continued)

SURVEY LEVEL	Operator Comments
Fugitives	
Stream type (gas, heavy oil, light oil, or water/oil)	
Average VOC weight %	
Number of components that handle the stream type	
Glycol Dehydrator Unit	
Processed throughput	
Glycol type	
Hours operated	
Gas saturated (yes/no)	
Unprocessed natural gas concentrations	
Equipped with a flash tank (yes/no)	
Disposition of flash gas	
Loading Operations	
Volume loaded to ships and barges	
Tank color	
Tank condition	
Losses from Flashing	
Type of vessel	
API gravity of stored oil	

B-8

GOADS-2005 QA Summary Form Data Fields (Continued)

SURVEY LEVEL	Operator Comments
Operating pressure of each vessel	
Operating temperature of each vessel	
Operating pressure upstream of vessel	
Operating temperature upstream of vessel	
Oil/condensate throughput for each vessel	
Disposition of flash gas	
Mud Degassing	
Number of drilling days (with mud)	
Mud type used (water-based, synthetic, oil-based)	
Natural Gas Turbines	
Hours operated	
Operating horsepower	
Maximum rated fuel usage	
Average fuel usage	
Control device identified	
Same equipment units reported for each month/survey	
Natural Gas Engines	
Engine stroke	
Engine burn	

GOADS-2005 QA Summary Form Data Fields (Continued)

SURVEY LEVEL	Operator Comments
Hours operated	
Operating horsepower	
Maximum rated fuel usage	
Average fuel usage	
Control device identified	
Same equipment units reported for each month/survey	
Pneumatic Pumps	
Manufacturer	
Model	
Hours operated	
Pressure/level Controllers	
Manufacturer	
Model	
Hours operated	
Service type	
Storage Tank	
Product throughput	
Product type	
Tank color	

GOADS-2005 QA Summary Form Data Fields (Continued)

SURVEY LEVEL	Operator Comments
Tank condition	
Tank shape	
Tank orientation	
Tank shell height	
Tank shell diameter	
Tank shell width	
Roof shape	
Roof height above shell	
Equipped with a flash tank (yes/no)	
Cold Vent	
Hours operated, including upsets	
Volume vented, including upsets	
Control device identified	
Average vent feed	

* If the uncontrolled quantity emitted from the amine unit is not completed.

The Department of the Interior Mission

As the Nation's principal conservation agency, the Department of the Interior has responsibility for most of our nationally owned public lands and natural resources. This includes fostering sound use of our land and water resources; protecting our fish, wildlife, and biological diversity; preserving the environmental and cultural values of our national parks and historical places; and providing for the enjoyment of life through outdoor recreation. The Department assesses our energy and mineral resources and works to ensure that their development is in the best interests of all our people by encouraging stewardship and citizen participation in their care. The Department also has a major responsibility for American Indian reservation communities and for people who live in island territories under U.S. administration.

The Minerals Management Service Mission

As a bureau of the Department of the Interior, the Minerals Management Service's (MMS) primary responsibilities are to manage the mineral resources located on the Nation's Outer Continental Shelf (OCS), collect revenue from the Federal OCS and onshore Federal and Indian lands, and distribute those revenues.

Moreover, in working to meet its responsibilities, the **Offshore Minerals Management Program** administers the OCS competitive leasing program and oversees the safe and environmentally sound exploration and production of our Nation's offshore natural gas, oil and other mineral resources. The MMS **Minerals Revenue Management** meets its responsibilities by ensuring the efficient, timely and accurate collection and disbursement of revenue from mineral leasing and production due to Indian tribes and allottees, States and the U.S. Treasury.

The MMS strives to fulfill its responsibilities through the general guiding principles of: (1) being responsive to the public's concerns and interests by maintaining a dialogue with all potentially affected parties and (2) carrying out its programs with an emphasis on working to enhance the quality of life for all Americans by lending MMS assistance and expertise to economic development and environmental protection.

www.ingramcontent.com/pod-product-compliance
Lightning Source LLC
Chambersburg PA
CBHW052006280526
45793CB00005B/871